Held in contempt

MANCHESTER
1824

Manchester University Press

Held in contempt

contempt

What's wrong with the House of Commons?

Hannah White

Manchester University Press

Published by Manchester University Press
Oxford Road, Manchester M13 9PL

www.manchesteruniversitypress.co.uk

British Library Cataloguing-in-Publication Data
A catalogue record for this book is available from the British Library

ISBN   978 1 5261 5669 3   paperback

First published 2022

Typeset
by New Best-set Typesetters Ltd
Printed in Great Britain
by Bell & Bain Ltd, Glasgow

Contents

Foreword

When I sat down to write this book in early 2020, I felt I had plenty of evidence of what was wrong with the House of Commons – in particular the ways in which its complex governance and procedures, combined with the exceptionalist attitude of MPs, were damaging public trust in parliament. Sadly, two incidents – which occurred too late to be incorporated fully into the text of this book – have provided further evidence to support my argument.

In late 2021, a scandal broke which epitomised the exceptionalism I describe in chapter four – the implicit belief held by too many MPs that there should be one rule for them and another for the rest of us. 'Partygate' – the revelation that politicians and civil servants working in Whitehall during the Covid-19 pandemic had held social gatherings in contravention of the lockdown rules they themselves had set for the rest of the population – rocked Westminster and cut through to the public like few previous scandals.

It is unclear as yet what the legal or political consequences of this rule-breaking will be, but in terms of public trust in politics, the impact of partygate is already very clear. Primed by the autumn 2021 scandal over paid lobbying by Conservative MP Owen Paterson, and the efforts of his party colleagues to dismantle the Commons standards system which had determined his guilt, many members of the public had already been reminded of their low opinion of MPs. But with allegations about parties breaching Covid-19 regulations going right to the top of government, the belief that some MPs think the rules they set for others should not apply to them has become even more firmly embedded in the public mind.

As I write in my conclusion, 'Every reported misdemeanour by an individual MP, every example of MPs acting as if rules do not apply to them, chips away at public respect for the House of Commons in a way which is not easy to repair.' Partygate is the latest and most egregious example of an incident contributing to the spiral of public contempt for the House of Commons.

Second, in early 2022, MPs chose to corroborate the argument I make in chapter 5, about the problems of governance, short-termism and executive dominance which have hampered efforts to restore the Palace of Westminster, including the latest 'Restoration and Renewal' project. In that chapter, I discuss how the parliamentary convention that no parliament can bind its successors 'means that no decision about the project – even the law passed to establish the Sponsor Board and Delivery Authority – can ever be regarded as final, because it could always be superseded by a subsequent decision.'

This turns out to have been a prescient observation. In February 2022, the House of Commons Commission – the body of MPs and officials which administers the House – announced its recommendation that MPs should abolish the independent Sponsor Body (which they had previously established in law) in order to take decisions about the renovation back into the hands of MPs and peers. This decision was the consequence of the Sponsor Body's unwelcome persistence in arguing – in line with the findings of numerous previous reviews but against prevailing political preferences – that it would be too expensive and dangerous for parliamentarians to remain on the estate while the restoration of the Palace took place.

And so has begun the latest chapter in the history of attempts to restore the Palace of Westminster – 'the litany of dithering, buck-passing and delay which illustrates many of the themes ... discussed in this book.'

Hannah White
Brighton, February 2022

Acknowledgements

My greatest debt in the writing of this book is to Jenny McCullough – for her encouragement, expertise, willingness to read my early drafts and clerkly eye for detail (although all errors are mine).

Grateful thanks also to Sarah Childs, Peter Riddell, Ben Page, Alex Meakin, Martyn Atkins, Roger Mortimore, Adam Wagner and members of the Study of Parliament Group. The book has benefitted from the reflections and insights of many parliamentarians past and present – thanks in particular to Sarah Wollaston, Pete Wishart, Charles Walker and Hilary Benn as well as to others who preferred not to be named. To my colleagues at the House of Commons and the Institute for Government – I'm endlessly grateful for your ideas, insight and advice.

Thanks to everyone at Manchester University Press. I'm grateful to Jon de Peyer for encouraging me to write this book in the first place, and to Emma Brennan for keeping me going.

Acknowledgements

I could not have written this book without the forbearance and encouragement of my wonderful family and the sanity-check of the 'fascinating women'. But my deepest gratitude is to my amazing parents, without whose unstinting love, kindness and support I would be nowhere – thank you.

Introduction

On the last Wednesday of August 2019, as the UK raced towards the Prime Minister's 31 October deadline for taking the UK out of the EU, Boris Johnson asked the Queen to shut down parliament. For a month, a constitutional argument raged about whether the Prime Minister was misusing his powers by 'proroguing'[1] parliament for five weeks. The matter was settled in late September by the eleven justices of the Supreme Court, who found the suspension to be 'unlawful, void and of no effect'.[2] The court ruled that Boris Johnson's prorogation would have prevented parliament from carrying out its constitutional functions without any reasonable justification.

The day after the court judgment, parliamentarians returned to Westminster and all traces of the prorogation were – literally – erased from the records of the House of Commons. But what could not be expunged so readily was the clear message from the Prime Minister to the public – that in the run-up to the most significant change in the UK's constitutional status for decades, it did not matter if parliament was absent. In the government's eyes, parliament was unimportant, except as a mechanism to deliver its key policy objective – to 'get Brexit done'. Worse, parliament was an impediment to government delivering on the will of the people, a narrative that Johnson and his ministers repeatedly hammered home in the months that followed. This was ironic given the weight that Johnson and other Brexit supporters had placed on parliament 'taking back control' of its sovereignty during the referendum campaign.

Post-Brexit, the government narrative of parliamentary insignificance has increasingly been reflected in reality. Despite the repatriation of powers from MEPs in Brussels to MPs in Westminster, the overall effect of the UK's exit from the European Union (EU) has been a significant transfer of power from parliament to government. Ministers have accrued broad and deep powers to change the statute book with minimal parliamentary scrutiny. And they can shape swathes of domestic policy – from agriculture to immigration – via trade negotiations in which parliament has almost no role.[3]

This strengthening of the executive at the expense of parliament has since been reinforced by the UK government's response to the Covid-19 pandemic, in which ministers have frequently rendered the legislature a bystander. In the early days of the crisis – when a speedy response was essential – this was understandable, but as the months passed it became increasingly less so. From the public's perspective parliament's role in the pandemic response has been barely perceptible, and the House of Commons has been largely impotent to resist a massive transfer of power away from the legislature and towards the executive. Over the same period, public contempt for the Commons has been exacerbated by scandals about bullying, sexual harassment, paid lobbying, second jobs and lockdown parties.

Tales of the decline of Westminster's parliament are not new. Academics and commentators have worried for over a century about the imbalance of power between a weak legislature and an over-mighty executive, and the consequences for parliament's effectiveness and public trust in the institution. In recent decades, that story has been challenged by a more nuanced account – highlighting the subtle ways in which parliament influences government 'off stage' and parliamentarians work in private to force ministers to compromise in order to avoid high-profile defeats in parliament. But while this work has provided a much more accurate picture of the power dynamics which shape parliament behind the scenes, the public's view has been of a legislature scorned by the government and careless of its own reputation.

In this book, I explore the unprecedented twin challenges presented for Westminster by Brexit and Covid-19, in the context of longer-term problems with the way the House of Commons functions. In some ways, these exceptional events have illustrated parliament operating entirely as expected – with front-of-house debates and votes, and behind-the-scenes dealing and influence. But in other ways these two crises have both highlighted and exacerbated worrying trends – government's increasing use of fast-track processes to make laws in ways which minimise parliament's role, and ministers' disregard for scrutiny and their disinclination to update inadequate parliamentary processes, the shortcomings of which operate in their favour. These trends in government behaviour are contributing to low public trust, which itself is damaged by the exceptionalism and unrepresentativeness of MPs and the arcane nature of parliamentary procedures – themes which I explore in later chapters.

It is tempting to view what has happened in parliament during Brexit and Covid-19 as exceptional circumstances which can safely be set aside as aberrations. But in this book, I argue to the contrary. While the events of the last decade may have been unusual, we should pay close attention to what they tell us about the health of our parliamentary democracy. There is a danger that these periods of exception have reinforced existing problems and normalised new patterns of political behaviour which will become entrenched as the norm. The risk is that the experience of dealing with Brexit and Covid-19 has reinforced a vicious cycle of decline in Westminster – of executive disregard for parliament, which undermines public trust in its role, and in turn further emboldens ministers to side-line the legislature, damaging parliament's ability to play its part in our democracy. We must recognise the vicious cycle into which Westminster has fallen and find ways to reverse the decline – setting up a virtuous circle which nurtures greater public trust in and executive respect for parliament's role. Otherwise, I believe we risk the inevitable decline of our key democratic institution.

The role of the House of Commons

What role does parliament play and why should we value it? Since it first came into existence in the thirteenth century, as a means for the monarch to raise money and armies in return for addressing the grievances of the most prominent citizens of the day, the House of Commons has played a crucial part in mediating between government and the people – representing the interests of the public while enabling ministers chosen from among its numbers to govern. By the start of the nineteenth century, following the Acts of Union with Scotland and Ireland, the House of Commons of the United Kingdom of Great Britain and Ireland had largely evolved into the institution we would recognise today, fulfilling four core roles: enabling the government to pass laws; holding it to account for its decisions and actions; providing a forum for national debate; and representing the views and concerns of constituents.

While its procedures are far from perfect, the House of Commons today provides important checks and balances on the actions of people in power – whether officials or politicians. Among all the individuals and bodies that scrutinise government, only MPs can quiz the Prime Minister every week, require ministers to answer questions every day and demand a response to their questions and conclusions.[4] When done well, scrutiny increases the chances of government failures being identified (and avoids their repetition), allows the concerns of the public to be raised and enables new policy ideas to emerge from outside government. Only parliament can shape the laws which governments seek to introduce, improving the quality of the legislation that governs our lives. And while our national debate has increasingly shifted out of the Commons chamber and into newsrooms, column inches and the online platforms of new forms of media, the legislature can still provide a focal point for debates on issues that are central to the interests of the country.

Beyond these practical functions, the House of Commons also plays a crucial symbolic role. Under the so-called 'Westminster system' ('invented' in England and then exported around the Commonwealth), the elected House provides legitimacy to the government of the day. UK governments are led by the leader of the party with the greatest number of elected MPs and composed of ministers drawn mainly from among their number (along with an occasional sprinkling of unelected peers). A government can only continue to govern if it 'commands the confidence' of the House of Commons, meaning it can win a majority of votes for its key policies. In this way Westminster is different to other democratic systems in which the government and legislature are elected separately and so have individual mandates from the electorate – and a separate source of legitimacy.

The House of Commons' role in underpinning the government is one of the key reasons why it matters that Westminster has fallen into a vicious cycle of declining public trust and executive contempt. If the public see the Commons as incompetent, as irrelevant or as failing to represent their interests, then the government from which it is drawn will also see its reputation suffer. If government is seen as inappropriately controlling and dominating of parliament, then the public will not have confidence that the checks and balances of parliamentary scrutiny are operating as they should, and may rightly distrust the government or suspect it of using its powers inappropriately. And if the Commons is seen as an outdated institution which is resistant to reform of the way it runs itself, with one set of rules for MPs and another for everyone else, then members of the public are justified in asking why they should allow the way they live their lives to be dictated by the regulations and laws that MPs pass. If proof were needed, the Covid-19 pandemic has demonstrated just how important it is for the public to have confidence in government and to be willing to obey the rules which MPs ask us all to follow.

The importance of public trust in the House of Commons

The vicious cycle of parliamentary decline exacerbated by Brexit and Covid-19 might be less consequential in a context in which parliament's public reputation was strong and its role in society was respected. Unfortunately, neither is true. Although public contempt for MPs has long been a feature of UK politics – post-war Labour leader Hugh Gaitskell noted as far back as 1954 that his profession was 'looked upon in many quarters as a slightly odd, somewhat discreditable, rather silly occupation'[5] – levels of trust have declined dramatically in recent decades. Public trust in the House of Commons is now at an all-time low, and lower than that enjoyed by most other European parliaments.

The best sources of long-term, comparative data on public attitudes to the UK's national parliament come from the EU – the Eurobarometer, European Values Study and European Social Survey have been tracking trust in the national parliaments of the EU and other national and European institutions since 1973, 1981 and 2002, respectively. These surveys allow us to compare levels of trust between different institutions within the UK and in parliaments across European countries.[6]

The European Values Study suggests that in the three decades between 1981 and 1984, when it was first conducted, and the most recent survey (administered between 2008 and 2010), confidence in the British parliament dropped by 17 per cent, from 41 per cent to just 24 per cent. To some extent, low and falling public trust in legislatures is not unusual internationally. Some other countries, including Germany and Norway, experienced similar falls to the UK over the same period, although in the most recent survey, over 60 per cent of Norwegians still said they were confident in their parliament compared to only 24 per cent of British interviewees. But the downward trend in the UK has not been universal across European countries. Citizens of Belgium, Italy, Spain and Denmark all became more confident in their national parliaments over the thirty-year period to 2010, with confidence in the Danish parliament climbing over 30 percentage points.[7]

The fact that, by 2010, fewer than one in four of the UK public had confidence in their parliament might seem bad, but in subsequent years, trust fell further still. By 2019, according to the Eurobarometer, levels of confidence in the UK parliament among the UK public had dropped to just 19 per cent – fewer than one in five Britons 'tended to trust' their national parliament.

Among all European legislatures, the UK parliament is now one of the least trusted. In the 2019 Eurobarometer, more than three times as many Danes, Finns, Netherlanders and Luxembourgers expressed a high or fair degree of trust in their legislature as Britons did in their own parliament (68, 64, 64 and 62 per cent, respectively, compared to 19 per cent). The average level of trust across all European countries – 34 per cent – was nearly twice as high as in the UK; only citizens of Bulgaria (17 per cent) and Hungary (13 per cent) had less trust in their parliament.

As well as faring badly in relation to other European legislatures, the UK parliament is held in low esteem among other UK institutions. Again, this is not atypical – according to international surveys, national parliaments tend to be among the least trusted institutions in most countries.[8] But even within this set of distrusted institutions, the UK parliament does particularly badly. The 2019 Eurobarometer figure of 19 per cent put the Westminster parliament and the British government jointly second lowest of all the UK institutions the public was asked about, ahead only of political parties (on 8 per cent). Parliament and government were both far behind the army (trusted by 80 per cent of the public), the police (74 per cent), the justice system (57 per cent) and local public authorities (47 per cent). Even though the survey was conducted in the middle of the Brexit crisis, more Britons said they tended to trust the EU (29 per cent) and the European parliament (35 per cent) than their own parliament.

Many politicians assume that trust in politicians and political institutions has always been low and there is not much anyone can do about it. But the comparative data from the Eurobarometer survey show that low levels of public trust in parliament are not an inevitable fact of life. Yes, distrust of national parliaments is widespread, but levels of trust vary significantly between countries. And some countries have succeeded in increasing levels of trust in their parliament over time.

What shapes public trust in the House of Commons?

The task of reversing the vicious cycle of executive disregard and falling public trust into which Westminster has fallen is not an impossible one. But in order to approach this task, we need to understand the factors shaping public perceptions of the House of Commons. MPs themselves play a vital role in shaping how the Commons is seen. In some ways this is obvious; it was easy to see the impact on public trust of weeks of *Daily Telegraph* headlines about members' misuse of their expenses. But in this book, I also examine other ways in which the actions or inaction of MPs are corroding public trust in our key democratic institution. The philosopher Onora O'Neill argues that institutions need to provide evidence that they are competent, reliable or honest to persuade the public that they should have trust in them.[9] In my view, MPs too readily provide the public with evidence that they should not.

But – although this book focuses in large part on the role played by politicians in shaping public perceptions of their own institution – low levels of public trust in parliament are not simply the result of the actions of MPs and peers. Although scandals and high-profile crises have caused identifiable drops in public confidence, parliament's 'trust problem' must be seen in the wider context of socio-political and technological changes which have affected the reputation and standing of most public institutions in the UK and internationally. A major study published in 2020 by the Bennett Institute for Public Policy at the University of Cambridge found that globally, youth satisfaction with democracy has been declining – not only in absolute terms, but also relative to how older generations felt at the same stages in life.[10] The historian Anne Applebaum situates the decline in trust in institutions across the United States and Europe as one aspect of the polarisation of politics in the decades since the fall of the Berlin Wall, which she argues has led 'from the fragmentation of the public sphere, to the absence of a center ground, from the rise of partisanship to the waning influence of respected neutral institutions'.[11] The UK parliament is not the only institution seeing its reputation decline.

The reputation of parliament has been significantly shaped over time by the attentions of the UK's active press and broadcast media. The country's tabloid and broadsheet newspapers have long seen parliament as a useful source of stories to sate their appetite for scandal and slurs. The emergence, during the 1990s, of the 24-hour news cycle– driven first by cable television and subsequently by social media – put a further premium on news – preferably bad news – in order to secure audience share and advertiser revenue. The academic and peer Philip Norton has noted the cumulative effect of traditional media and new social channels. 'Deference to parliament has been undermined', he argues, 'by popular cynicism, a less interested and less informed media, and the emergence of social media, all of which have contributed to a more distracted population, one wanting instant gratification, and with a short attention span.'[12] Whatever useful and positive work parliamentarians might be doing, the media's preference for scandal makes it difficult for MPs and peers to promote a positive view of their institution.

Public trust in parliament has also been shaped by changes in the UK's structures and processes of government. The past half-century has seen a reduction in parliament's significance caused by changes to its role and responsibilities. What the political journalist Peter Riddell diagnosed in 1998 as the most significant challenge to parliament – its 'growing irrelevance ... to the main decisions affecting people's lives'[13] – has grown more serious since. Riddell argued that parliament was losing its importance because other institutions were encroaching upon its responsibilities, and it was failing to cope with the growth of alternative centres of power including the EU, the judiciary, the media, regulators and quangos. Policy decisions that would previously have been debated in Westminster were now taken in Brussels, political debates were held in broadcast studios rather than the Commons chamber, judges were expanding their role in interpreting the actions of government, and an increasing proportion of public services were delivered by quangos, blurring lines of accountability to MPs. All these changes diminished the importance of parliament.

In the twenty years since Riddell was writing, a massive extension of devolution has further circumscribed Westminster's role, reducing its significance in the eyes of the public. The power to make laws and deliver public services across a broad range of policy areas has been given away to governments in Scotland, Wales, to the power-sharing executive in Northern Ireland (as part of the Good Friday Agreement) and – in a more limited way – to mayors in different parts of England. New legislatures have been established to scrutinise the devolved administrations and the purview of the House of Commons has shrunk proportionately. For the over ten million UK citizens not living in England, many decisions taken in Westminster have become irrelevant – as became abundantly clear during the Covid-19 pandemic, during which health, education and welfare policies between the UK's four governments diverged.[14]

Linked to the expansion of devolution, the more frequent use of referendums has mounted a challenge to the unquestioned primacy of parliamentary representative democracy as a means of deciding national questions.[15] Asking the public to decide directly about contentious issues inevitably shifts the focus of democratic engagement away from parliament and towards the people. This may be a positive thing if it increases public participation in decision-making or enhances the legitimacy of key policy decisions, but, as the Independent Commission on Referendums convened by the UCL Constitution Unit concluded, we should also 'be mindful of the risks of undermining [our system of representative democracy]' posed by the use of referendums.[16] As I explore later, the 2016 EU referendum created particular tensions between representative and direct democracy: some Remain voters criticised MPs for delegating the decision on EU membership to the people at all, while inconclusive parliamentary debates over the future UK–EU relationship left some Leave supporters concerned that MPs might not implement the referendum outcome at all.

Public trust in parliament, then, is shaped by a wide range of factors – from the local and singular to the international and secular. There can be no single, simple solution to the downward spiral of distrust and executive disdain into which Westminster has fallen. But just because many of the political, social and technological trends I have described may be beyond the control of individual MPs, that does not mean that they can be absolved of responsibility for addressing problems with the House of Commons itself.

When they first arrive in Westminster, many new MPs are acutely conscious of the anachronisms and oddities of parliament. But this is also the moment when they are most inexperienced and least equipped to challenge how things are done. Their desire to challenge tends to dissipate quickly as they are indoctrinated by more experienced colleagues into the longstanding status quo. 'The system is designed to crush anything innovative and new', Sarah Wollaston MP told me shortly before the election in which she lost her Totnes seat. 'When I first arrived, a colleague advised me to wait a couple of years and the procedures would all make perfect sense … but they still don't.' Before long, most MPs are so occupied by working on behalf of their constituents and fulfilling the multiple overlapping responsibilities of being an elected member, that they have little time to think about strengthening the House of Commons itself. Nor – because they each have their own individual electoral mandate – do they have any collective sense of responsibility to the institution of which they are part. These factors conspire to inhibit MPs from addressing fundamental problems which undermine the reputation of the House of Commons.

This book

If the House of Commons is to continue fulfilling its important roles, it must reverse the downward spiral of public distrust which is contributing to the weakening of its role in our system of government. It is surprising that MPs are not more concerned about the declining influence of the Commons. As the veteran Conservative MP Kenneth Clarke commented in 2019, 'In my opinion, in recent years this House has seen a considerable diminution of its powers and has often seemed rather indifferent to the eroding of some of the powers we used to have to hold governments to account.'[17] Parliamentary scrutiny is only effective if a government feels it needs to engage with the process and with its outcomes. If the public does not value our legislature, then governments will feel emboldened to avoid scrutiny and ignore its recommendations.

There are worrying signs that this is starting to happen. In recent years there has been a growing tendency for governments to treat law-making as a 'tick-box' process, passing legislation as fast as possible, introducing 'skeleton' bills with minimal detail and creating sweeping powers to allow themselves to fill in the detail at a later date. That means important aspects of policy are set using secondary legislation which receives minimal parliamentary oversight.[18] In Chapter 1, I discuss how this habit, which was already forming before Brexit, was reinforced by the need to pass swathes of new laws rapidly before the UK left the EU. The Covid-19 pandemic has put this trend on steroids – with the public health emergency used to justify minimal, retrospective scrutiny of regulations that have imposed draconian restrictions on the freedoms of the UK population.

Both the Brexit period and the pandemic have also raised fundamental questions about the role of MPs and whether they should act as the representatives or delegates of those who elect them. In Chapter 2, I discuss the implications of the fact that House of Commons itself is not descriptively representative of the population it serves. This raises questions about the extent to which MPs can substantively represent the interests of under-represented groups. There is also a serious risk that the anachronistic working practices and the physical constraints of the parliamentary estate could slow or even reverse recent trends towards increased diversity of MPs. If trust in the House of Commons is to be justified, MPs need to make it a welcoming environment for the broadest range of people.

That may mean being prepared to question some of the key tenets which underpin their thinking about the House. Most MPs and many members of the public are understandably attached to the long history of the House of Commons, which has had a longer continuous existence than most other parliaments. Together the rituals, traditions, language and heritage of parliament lend gravitas and importance to the deliberations of MPs. But it is too easy to assume that a long history is a synonymous with contemporary superiority.[19] On the contrary, in some ways the long history of the Commons is a disadvantage. A new MP working out how to get things done must grapple with a complex web of temporary and permanent rules, precedents, conventions and Speakers' decisions which have accreted over centuries. This leads to an inequity between the MPs who have had (and taken) the time to learn the rules (or how to seek advice from those whose job it is to understand them) and those who have not. It also means that what goes on in the House of Commons can be an impenetrable mystery for those outside looking in. In Chapter 3 I argue that the rules by which the

Commons governs itself must be simplified to make its proceedings intelligible to the public.

As well as often privileging tradition over innovation, some MPs have a dangerous tendency towards exceptionalism. The doctrine of 'parliamentary sovereignty' (that parliament is the highest legal authority, the courts generally cannot overturn its legislation and no parliament can pass laws that future parliaments cannot change) leads some MPs to treat themselves as a class apart within the country they represent. This tendency, which I explore in Chapter 4, has repeatedly contributed to scandals which have undermined the reputation of the House of Commons. The behaviour which led to the expenses scandal, for example, was generated in part by the unspoken collective belief among MPs that normal rules about claiming expenses did not apply to them. The 'Pestminster' #MeToo scandal was enabled by the resistance of some MPs to normal HR procedures. Allegations of bullying and harassment could not be dealt with as they would have been in any other workplace due to 'a culture, cascading from the top down, of deference, subservience, acquiescence and silence'.[20] Most recently, the Johnson government's response to the paid lobbying undertaken by former Conservative minister Owen Paterson and the 'partygate' scandal have reinforced public perceptions that MPs have one rule for their friends and another for everyone else.

The exceptionalist culture of the House of Commons has also contributed to failures to safeguard its future. The constitutional reality that only MPs can make decisions about their own institution ensures that – where there is a conflict – the preferences of current MPs will always be privileged over the long-term interests of the House. This is the context for the decades-long failure to move ahead with the restoration of the Palace of Westminster. As I discuss in Chapter 5, the sorry history of this mega-infrastructure project exemplifies many of the problems I highlight in earlier chapters. The restoration has been opposed by successive generations of MPs unwilling either to move out of the palace or to take the political hit of having to justify its price tag to their constituents. Today's parliamentarians – who will bear all the risk, cost and inconvenience of the works – have no incentive to act in the interests of their successors twenty or thirty years in the future. Over time, their failure to act is not only multiplying the likelihood of a catastrophic accident, but also ratcheting up the eventual cost of the project and, in the process, undermining the reputation of the Commons.

Ironically, perhaps the failure of politicians to progress with the physical restoration of parliament will end up being the trigger that is needed for substantive reform of the institution. Regrettably, the history of the House of Commons and other legislatures, demonstrates that significant change only happens following a crisis. Without a 'burning platform', short-term political self-interest almost always stands in the way of building the long-term effectiveness of the institution. Brexit and Covid-19 have both posed significant challenges to parliament but neither has created a crisis in the institution itself. Nor has the catastrophic decline in trust in the House of Commons prompted serious attention, let alone action from our political class. Perhaps it is only a major crisis in parliament itself – a literal conflagration which forces MPs and peers out of Westminster or a scandal going to the very root of the institution – which could be significant enough to jolt politicians into acknowledging the shortcomings of the way we are currently 'doing' politics. Perhaps it is only a disaster which can reverse the cycle of decline into which Westminster has fallen.

Side-lined

Introduction

At 5 p.m. on Wednesday 10 June 2020, seventeen MPs met in the wood-panelled and flock-wallpapered surroundings of Committee Room 11 in the Palace of Westminster. Carefully spaced around the room's ornate wooden pews in order to maintain the required social distance, the MPs were there to scrutinise a set of regulations – also known as 'delegated' or 'secondary' legislation – which would change the Covid-19 lockdown which the government had imposed seven weeks before.

The regulations which the Care Minister, Helen Whately MP, invited the members of the committee to approve that Wednesday began loosening the lockdown – allowing people to exercise with another person or to leave home for recreation, reopening household waste sites, garden centres and outdoor sports facilities, permitting goods to be collected from shops and facilitating the process of moving house.[1]

The public health legislation which gave the government the power to impose the lockdown – the Public

Health (Control of Diseases) Act 1984 – dictated that in normal circumstances, regulations like these should not take effect before they had been approved by both the Commons and the Lords. But when drafting the Act, ministers had anticipated the possibility of circumstances in which a swifter response might be required and a delay to allow for parliamentary scrutiny might cost lives. The Act therefore included a special 'urgency provision'. This enabled ministers to make new laws without prior parliamentary approval.

For these lockdown regulations, and most of the others it made using powers in the 1984 Act, the government made use of this urgency procedure. By declaring he was 'of the opinion that, by reason of urgency, it is necessary to make the order without a draft being so laid and approved' the then Secretary of State for Health and Social Care, Matt Hancock MP, and later his successor Sajid Javid MP, were able to bring the regulations into force before they had even been formally shown to parliament, let alone approved.

This meant that the regulations the committee considered on 10 June were actually already in force – they had been 'made' by Matt Hancock on 12 May and had come into effect that midnight. They were then 'laid' before parliament at 9.30 a.m. the following day, at which point they were published on www.legislation.gov.uk. So it was not until nine and a half hours after the regulations had started to operate that MPs and the public could even read the law to which they were already subject.

For regulations made using this special 'urgency' procedure to continue to operate, they have to be approved by a committee of each House within 28 days. But having made the changes it wanted to the law on 13 May, the government was in no hurry to allow parliament to scrutinise what it had done. The government whips did not arrange committee meetings to approve the regulations until after the law had been operating for nearly four weeks.

In fact, it was worse than that. Not only had the law been operating for nearly a month by the time the Commons committee met on 10 June, but the debate also took place only *after the regulations had already been superseded* by further legislation. New regulations that came into effect on 1 June – also without prior scrutiny – had lifted the lockdown and replaced it with an overnight residence requirement. By the time the equivalent Lords committee met to consider the regulations on 12 June, yet another set of new regulations had been made, reopening all shops and introducing support 'bubbles'. Justin Madders, the Labour MP who spoke for the opposition in the Commons committee, described the delay in scrutiny as 'frankly an insult' to parliament.

And this was not a one-off occurrence. What started as understandable delays caused by a government moving at speed to respond to an emerging threat, rapidly became a habit.[2] Routine and lengthy delays in parliamentary scrutiny of Covid-19 regulations became the norm. This was problematic for several reasons. First, it created an accountability gap. Ministers were bringing in draconian provisions and changing criminal laws relating to the lockdown, with significant consequences for people's lives, simply by signing a piece of paper. Second, the delays reduced the chances of errors in the legislation being picked up and rectified before laws came into effect. The risk of such errors was increased by the fact that regulations were introduced and then – rather than being replaced – were repeatedly amended over time: these amendments meant that they grew from 11 pages in length on 26 March to over 130 pages at the end of the last lockdown. Without timely opportunities to debate the changes in parliament, mistakes and contradictions were only picked up as the regulations were enforced.[3] Third, delayed scrutiny meant that the police and the public did not have time to read and understand the regulations before they came into force. As the regulations were amended again and again, they became more and more complex and difficult to decipher. 'Lawyers have thrown their hands up in the air and have said "we just don't know what they mean"', said the human rights barrister Adam Wagner six months into the pandemic in September 2020. 'Police I have spoken to say they have just given up. They say there is no way they can enforce the rules like this.'[4] The public were confused too.

By autumn 2020, the continued use of the urgency procedure to bring new lockdown laws into effect without parliamentary scrutiny was becoming less and less justifiable. As the Lords Constitution Committee argued in a 2021 report on Covid-19 and emergency powers:

> All governments should recognise that, however great or sudden an emergency may be, exceptional powers are

lent, not granted, by the legislature to the executive, and such powers should be returned as swiftly and completely as possible, avoiding any spill over into permanence.[5]

But the government showed no inclination to stop using these powers and MPs and peers had no effective way of challenging what had become habitual government practice. As the pandemic wore on, the government started to give the public more notice of the headlines of forthcoming law changes – announcing upcoming shifts in press conferences and in the media. But the legal detail of often highly significant changes – which sometimes differed from public briefing – was often published just hours or minutes before the regulations came into force. By this point in the pandemic there was no good reason why those regulations could not have been laid before parliament in draft before the government wanted them to come into effect, in sufficient time for them to be understood and debated. But this did not happen. Absurdly, the regulations relating to the Christmas 2020 lockdown were made after parliament had risen for the holidays, so were only scrutinised when parliament returned in the New Year. The government refused requests for an earlier recall of parliament to allow for scrutiny.

The Covid-19 pandemic has been an unforeseen and exceptional event and few would dispute the need for government to act quickly to respond to the emerging threat. Where ministers did not have the legal powers they needed to impose restrictions on the population, it was appropriate that they take them and make use of them – drawing on developing scientific understanding of Covid-19 to try to prevent the population from spreading the virus and to protect citizens from suffering its ill-effects. But however exceptional the circumstances, government still has a responsibility to ensure that appropriate checks and balances – including parliamentary scrutiny – are retained where possible, and restored expeditiously when not.

Ministers have been too slow to return to the good practice of ensuring parliament has the opportunity to scrutinise the use of emergency powers during the Covid-19 pandemic. The pandemic has demonstrated how easy it is for ministers to get into the habit of using emergency powers – which make their lives easier by restricting scrutiny – and to get used to operating without the constraints of having to secure parliamentary approval for their decisions until after they have come into force. As the barrister and academic Tom Hickman QC has argued, the pandemic has 'demonstrated the flexibility of our constitutional arrangements, but not in a positive way. They have shown how fragile parliament's constitutional role is in relation to delegated legislation and how easily the government can turn down the accountability dial to something approaching zero.'[6]

As I discuss in this chapter, the temptation for ministers to minimise the role of parliament was well established before the pandemic. But there is now a danger that this period of exception has reinforced ministers' existing tendency to treat parliament as an inconvenient hurdle and normalised new patterns of political behaviour which are becoming entrenched as the norm. The risk is that Covid-19, like Brexit, has reinforced the vicious cycle of decline in Westminster – in which executive disregard for parliament undermines public trust in its role, and in turn further emboldens ministers to side-line the legislature. Downplaying the role that parliament plays in our system of government may be politically expedient for ministers under pressure, but its longer-term consequences for the credibility of the legislature should be of deep concern.[7]

What impact can parliament have on government?

The reality is that parliament can and does play an important role in our democracy, but its ability to fulfil that role may be damaged by governments who try to disregard it.

In the mid-twentieth century, many academics began to argue that the UK parliament was in decline – becoming impotent in the face of a dominant executive. Since then, this narrative has been debunked by plenty of evidence to the contrary – parliamentary scrutiny can and does affect the work of government.[8] Often this can be frustrating for ministers because it delays the implementation of a policy, forces an unwelcome shift of position or embarrasses them by identifying a failure. Arguably, it is precisely because parliament can be effective that government is sometimes tempted to imply it is unimportant or tell the public that the legislature is overstepping its remit.

So how does parliamentary impact work? For government, being 'held to account' by parliament can be an uncomfortable process, especially when a committee gives a minister or official an uncomfortable grilling or – worse – forces them to resign. Such impact can be front-page news – as when the Conservative Home Secretary Amber Rudd MP was forced to step down after misleading the Home Affairs Committee over Windrush. High-profile scrutiny can force the government to do something it has set its face against – as when backbench and opposition pressure (led from outside parliament by the footballer Marcus Rashford) forced Boris Johnson to provide support for children eligible for free school meals in school holidays during the Covid-19 pandemic.

But the impact of parliament on government is not always box-office stuff. Select committees are an effective mechanism for generating low-key but important improvements in government. [9] Analysis by the Health Select Committee in the mid-2000s helped make the case to ban smoking in public places. The Covid-19 pandemic has yielded examples of MPs extracting information from officials, ministers and scientists that would not otherwise have been on the public record. And a particular strength of committees is when they move neglected issues higher on the government's agenda – as the Home Affairs Committee did in 2013 when it highlighted the problem of child sexual exploitation, or as the Environmental Audit Committee did with its work on microplastics in 2016.

The academic Meg Russell has argued that although the impact of parliament may sometimes be hard to discern, this is because much of its impact is pre-emptive – persuading ministers not to pursue a policy or to make a decision for fear of 'what the select committee might say'. And when they do make changes, ministers do not always acknowledge the influence that select committees have had on them, preferring to take the credit themselves.

According to analysis by Russell and Meghan Benton, approximately 40 per cent of the recommendations made by a sample of Commons select committees from 1997 to 2010 were accepted by government.[10] Although it gives us a general sense, this is not a terribly meaningful statistic – as the authors themselves acknowledge – because not all recommendations are equal: some would involve major policy reversals while others are simply tweaks to existing policies. But they found that even a third of recommendations calling for more significant policy changes were successful.[11]

Away from the committee corridor, activity in the Commons chamber can have an impact on government. Often the most significant policy changes are generated by backbench rebellions on the government's own side – as Boris Johnson found despite his 80-seat majority. In the year following the 2019 election, numerous policy reversals, including on the involvement of the Chinese firm Huawei in the UK's 5G network, visa charges for NHS workers and the method used to award A-level results to students in England and Wales, were either initiated or strongly supported by government backbenchers.

Then there are the decisions the government would like to make but cannot without parliamentary sign off. Decisions to commit UK troops overseas must be ratified by a vote in the House of Commons, for example.[12] This is not simply a formality – in August 2013 David Cameron's motion authorising military intervention in the Syrian civil war was defeated by 285 votes to 272, preventing him from deploying troops and leading President Obama to postpone proposed US action in the region. And in January 2017, the Supreme Court ruled that the government had to secure parliamentary authorisation – in the form of primary legislation – before using its prerogative powers to trigger the Article 50 process to withdraw the UK from the EU.[13]

When given the opportunity, parliament can make a significant contribution to the law-making process.[14] MPs and peers frequently identify inconsistencies, mistakes or unclear drafting which can then be rectified by government lawyers. Particularly when legislation is drafted and passed at speed in an emergency, scrutiny can be an important mechanism for picking up things that have been forgotten or overlooked. For example, the Coronavirus Act, which was passed rapidly as the UK went into its first lockdown in March 2020, was clarified to ensure that Jews and Muslims would not be cremated against their wishes, a risk created by the emergency powers given to local authorities to deal with a dramatic increase in fatalities.

Sometimes parliament's interventions on legislation are more high-profile: all recent Prime Ministers – even those with large majorities – have suffered defeats in the course of trying to pass laws. In 2005, Tony Blair lost a vote on a measure to allow terrorist suspects to be held for 90 days without charge; in 2009, Gordon

Brown was forced to drop provisions from a bill on parliamentary standards; and, in 2015, secondary legislation introduced by David Cameron to slash tax credits was delayed by the House of Lords until the government introduced a compensation scheme for the lowest paid.[15] Theresa May was not defeated during the 2016–17 parliament, but after she sacrificed her majority in the 2017 election she lost 33 divisions in the House of Commons, many of which were on Brexit-related legislation. Between taking over in July 2019 and triggering a December election, Boris Johnson racked up 12 defeats.

Parliament also has a less obvious but nonetheless crucial impact on government – it lends legitimacy to its actions. The fact that legislation is scrutinised, that ministers are asked to justify their decisions and could potentially lose their jobs for providing inadequate answers, that policies are debated and defended, helps give the public confidence that the government is doing its job properly. Public trust in government is one of the fundamental building blocks of a stable and prosperous society. When ministers choose to undermine the role of parliament, they undermine their own ability to govern the country.

Ministers cannot ignore parliament, as the examples above show. But the government sometimes seems to overlook the ways in which involving parliament can enhance and underpin its efforts, and civil servants treat it as an annoying roadblock to be circumnavigated on the path towards the implementation of policies. The former Labour minister Hilary Benn MP told me: 'When I was a minister, parliament was seen as a bit of a nuisance and an irritation. It was never given priority – I had to explain to civil servants why it was important.'

The former Labour minister Harriet Harman MP has argued that, during her time in government, the civil service had an antagonistic approach to parliament that was detrimental to good law-making:

> I think there is too much of an adversarial approach to parliament from the civil service: ... seeing parliament as an obstacle, something that is there to be a problem when you try and get your legislation through. I think they should have embraced more the notion that you are putting it into the public domain in parliament and actually, parliament can improve it, and select committees can improve it, instead of driving the business of the House through. Often, backbenchers on one or the other side will be right, and the warning signs won't have been listened to.[16]

Ministers often seem keen to get away with the minimum possible scrutiny of legislation. For decades, lawyers and constitutional experts have expressed concern about the growing frequency with which governments have used emergency procedures to 'fast-track' primary legislation. Sometimes this is essential. During the suspension of devolved government in Northern Ireland, the UK parliament often had to legislate on behalf of the Assembly at the very last minute when talks between the political parties broke down against a hard deadline. And at the start of the Covid-19 pandemic primary legislation needed to be passed at speed to provide the government with powers to respond.

Emergency procedures exist for good reason, but as the Lords Constitution Committee argued in 2009:

'fast-tracking of normal parliamentary procedure should only occur where strictly necessary'.[17] This is because it can limit opportunities for parliamentary scrutiny, lead to errors in the law-making process, restrict the ability of outside organisations to influence new laws and increase the risk of bad legislation making it onto the statute book. This is why it is problematic that governments have found reasons to use fast-track procedures ever more frequently.

It is particularly unfortunate when constitutionally significant legislation is passed at speed – not least because parliament's specialist committees (including those on the constitution, human rights and delegated powers) may not have time to provide the two Houses with their expert analysis before a bill is passed. Two of the bills which gave effect to the UK's departure from the EU were egregious examples of key constitutional statutes being passed inappropriately fast. The EU (Withdrawal Agreement) Act 2020 – which effectively rewrote the UK's post-Brexit constitutional framework – was considered over the course of just a single month – the final version having been published only the day before it received its second reading in the Commons. Worse still, the European Union (Future Relationship) Act 2020 – which allowed for ratification of the EU–UK Trade and Cooperation Agreement – was introduced to and passed by the UK parliament in a single day, 30 December 2020, having been published only 24 hours before. To compare with two earlier bills which changed the UK's relationship with the EU in much more limited ways, the Maastricht Treaty was considered over a period of more than 400 days and MPs and peers spent 25 days scrutinising the Lisbon Treaty over a period of nearly 200 days.[18]

The limited time available for scrutiny of the two Brexit bills was the result of the UK and EU's decision to let Brexit negotiations go down to the wire, deprioritising the involvement of their respective parliaments in examining the deal. But while the UK government used the 31 December deadline to justify the lightning-fast passage of the bill in the few days remaining before the transition period expired, the EU chose to apply the treaty provisionally to allow the European parliament time to examine and ratify the deal. As the academic Jeff King has argued, the rapid passage of the Future Relationship Act was 'a political choice rather than legal or logistical necessity'.[19]

Another problematic aspect of the way that governments approach law-making is their increasingly frequent use of secondary, rather than primary, legislation – as discussed in the introduction to this chapter. Secondary legislation – made by ministers using powers given to them in primary legislation – receives much less scrutiny than its 'parent Act'. MPs can debate the text for just 90 minutes and parliamentarians cannot amend regulations – only reject them entirely. This happens so incredibly rarely that when it does it creates a major ruckus – as in 2015 when the Lords refused to agree to regulations that would have significantly reduced tax credits. The temerity of their lordships prompted the government to instigate a review of how 'more certainty and clarity' could be brought to the passage of secondary legislation.[20] From a parliamentary perspective, the problem is the reverse – it is almost impossible for MPs or peers to exert any influence at all over the increasing torrent of secondary legislation. But this is a problem that no government has the incentive to tackle – strengthened scrutiny could only disturb the flow of government law-making.

What has driven the trend towards government making greater use of secondary legislation? In the broadest terms it has been the result of the increasing complexity of modern government – and, in particular, the welfare state. Parliament simply does not have enough time to put every law through the more rigorous (although still not perfect) processes used for primary legislation. But more recently two forms of external time constraint have driven up the volume of secondary legislation still further – first, the Article 50 deadline for delivering Brexit and second, the imperative of responding rapidly to Covid-19. Both created circumstances in which there was insufficient time for government to pass primary legislation to achieve its goals, pushing it towards ever greater use of secondary legislation.

In other respects, however, the trend towards greater use of secondary legislation is down to government choice. A major factor has been governments' growing contentment with bringing bills to parliament before they have fully worked out the detail of the policies they wish to enact. Such so-called 'skeleton bills' set only an overarching policy framework in law, while providing ministers with powers to fill in the detail using delegated legislation. According to Lord Newby, the Liberal Democrat Leader in the House of Lords, skeleton bills often appear 'because the government have committed themselves to doing something and do not know quite what to do'.[21] The problem with skeleton bills is that they hand all the power over to the Executive; when the detail of the policies the government is enacting finally arrives – in regulations – parliament has no ability to amend them.

Skeleton bills often create so-called 'Henry VIII' powers – super-strength delegations that not only allow ministers to make new laws but also to amend existing primary legislation using secondary legislation. These sweeping powers allow ministers to change or even remove existing acts of parliament with only the minimal scrutiny that parliament's processes for secondary legislation afford. This means that a law that went through a full scrutiny process (in each House a debate on the principle of the bill, followed by line-by-line scrutiny in committee and up to two further amending stages) can be changed or abolished by a process involving almost no oversight from MPs and peers.

The tight timetable for passing the primary legislation needed for Brexit meant many of the bills required went through parliament in skeleton form. One Lords committee described the Haulage Permits and Trailer Registration Bill as 'wholly skeletal, more of a mission statement than legislation', and complained that the Immigration and Social Security Coordination (EU withdrawal) Bill contained a clause 'so lacking in any substance whatsoever that it cannot even be described as a skeleton'. [22] Most Brexit bills contained Henry VIII powers. In some cases, this was entirely sensible – the powers enabled government to make minor changes to existing laws to reflect the UK's new position outside the EU that would not have been worth the trouble of primary legislation. But in other instances, the powers allowed the government to make significant policy changes without proper scrutiny – for example using secondary legislation to remove EU state aid rules (determining what support the government could legally give to companies) from British law.[23]

The weakening of parliament's role in scrutinising legislation has been a secular trend over recent decades. By choosing not to include the detail of their policies in primary legislation and failing to address the inadequacies of processes for the scrutiny of secondary legislation, successive governments have signalled they are content with a weak level of parliamentary scrutiny over the business of government. This may make ministers' lives easier, but it also risks undermining public trust in their policies. It should give the rest of us cause for alarm.

And over the last five years – during Brexit and the Covid-19 pandemic – we have seen an acceleration in the minimisation of parliament's role in wider policy scrutiny as well as legislative scrutiny. To some extent this has been due to the unavoidable time constraints within which government has been operating, but it has also been a matter of political choice. Both the May and Johnson governments actively sought to avoid scrutiny of their policies wherever possible and to undermine the credibility of the legislature in order to achieve their own political ends – ultimately promoting a narrative of 'parliament versus the people'.

Theresa May tried to side-line parliament

Having become Prime Minister following David Cameron's resignation in 2016, Theresa May chose to exclude parliamentarians from influencing her negotiating objectives for the UK's exit from the EU. She announced key 'red lines' at the Conservative Party conference without providing an opportunity for them to be debated in parliament. Next, she had to be restrained by the Supreme Court from triggering the Article 50 process without legislative authority from parliament. These events were an ominous early harbinger of her attitude to parliamentary involvement in the Brexit process.

In the 2017 snap election, May sought a mandate to push through her vision of Brexit. The electorate declined to give it to her. The loss of her majority could have prompted May to engage more actively with parliament – to establish the parameters of a deal that MPs would support. Instead, she doubled down on her strategy of excluding them.

What began as her early, perhaps understandable protestation that she 'could not give a running commentary' to parliament on her negotiations with the EU, developed into a more concerted effort to frustrate parliament's efforts to fulfil its scrutiny role. May tried and failed to prevent MPs having a final vote on a deal. Once she reached a deal with the EU, she tried to use the pressure of the approaching Article 50 deadline to compel the Commons to support it. Her ministers refused to release government analysis that would have informed debate in parliament, including studies of the potential economic impact of Brexit on different sectors of the economy, and of the impact of a 'no-deal' exit. In the frenetic five-month period between November 2018 and April 2019, the government used its control of the Commons agenda to prevent opposition and backbench MPs from having any opportunity to decide what the Commons could discuss, lest they use that time to mount a challenge to her plans.

As May's majority was small when she became Prime Minister and non-existent following the 2017 election (after which she governed with a confidence and supply agreement with the Democratic Unionist Party), her attempts to exclude parliament from the Brexit process were often unsuccessful. Twice, ministers were forced to release government papers and legal advice against their will.[24] The second time, the Commons deemed the legal advice released by the government to be incomplete, which resulted in the extraordinary, unprecedented spectacle of her government being found 'in contempt' of parliament. MPs managed to secure a 'meaningful vote' on the withdrawal agreement by amending the EU (Withdrawal) Bill to require the government to put the deal into primary legislation. And MPs resisted the time pressure of the Article 50 process by twice forcing the government to seek an extension to the negotiating timetable.

In March 2019, after losing two 'meaningful votes' on her deal in the House of Commons, May made an impassioned statement in front of Number 10 in which she positioned herself on the side of the people and against MPs. '[O]f this I am absolutely sure,' she said, 'you the public have had enough. You are tired of the infighting. You are tired of the political games and the arcane procedural rows. Tired of MPs talking about nothing else but Brexit ... I agree. I am on your side. It is now time for MPs to decide.'[25] As the academic Meg Russell has observed, this statement had more than a tinge of populism about it.[26]

From the public's perspective, though, May had a point. By 2019, MPs had spent three years failing either to agree on a single form of Brexit which could be negotiated and delivered or – as some continued to hope – to secure either a second referendum or a reversal of the first. For a country used to the clear cut results of a first-past-the-post electoral system the parliamentary paralysis created by the combination of minority government and Brexit divisions was baffling. For those who believed they had delivered a clear instruction to MPs to take the UK out of the EU, the lack of progress was deeply frustrating. Leave supporters suspected that MPs were seeking a way to reverse the outcome of the referendum. Elements of the British press enthusiastically fuelled these suspicions – in April 2017, after Theresa May had called her snap election, the *Daily Mail's* headline screamed 'CRUSH THE SABOTEURS' – a reference to Remain-supporting MPs and peers.

May argued that the mandate of the referendum put a duty on MPs to support her particular vision of Brexit

– in not doing so, she suggested, they were illegitimately privileging their own views over those of the people.[27] She accused parliamentarians who had voted against her vision for Brexit of actually not wanting to leave the EU at all, an outcome which she said would potentially cause 'irreparable damage to public trust – not just in this generation of politicians, but to our entire democratic process'. In rows about what form Brexit should take, this became a familiar refrain – those rejecting a particular vision of the UK's future relationship with the EU accused their opponents of rejecting the result of the referendum altogether. Even fellow Leave supporters accused each other of rejecting 'the will of the people' when they disagreed about what Brexit should look like.

Boris Johnson deliberately pitted parliament against the people

The refrain of 'parliament versus the people', which pitted the legitimacy of elected MPs against the 'will of the people' as represented by the referendum result, was picked up with even greater enthusiasm by May's successor – Boris Johnson. He came into office in July 2019 on a promise to 'get Brexit done' and identified parliament as the main impediment to doing so. By this point (different) majorities of MPs were opposed to both the May deal and to a 'no deal' exit. Johnson's strategy was to persuade the public that the actions of MPs in resisting his interpretation of Brexit – which readily entertained a 'no-deal' exit – were illegitimate.

Boris Johnson had become Prime Minister following a Conservative leadership campaign in which Dominic Raab – the MP who would later become his Foreign Secretary – argued that it 'would be wrong to rule out any tool', including proroguing parliament, to ensure that the UK left the EU on 31 October with or without a deal.[28] In a televised debate between the leadership candidates – in which Boris Johnson declined to participate – four of Raab's rivals (two of whom went on to serve with him in Johnson's cabinet) condemned his threat against parliament. 'You don't deliver on democracy by trashing democracy', warned Sajid Javid – shortly to be Johnson's Chancellor. 'I think to suggest that you would suspend parliament and put an end to our sovereign democracy just ... to implement democracy is just not right, and we can't do that.'

One of Johnson's first actions as Prime Minister was to do exactly that, while the trenchant objections of certain new cabinet ministers curiously evaporated. Taking over the leadership of the country from Theresa May, just a few days before the summer recess, he made only a brief appearance before the Commons. Then, in the middle of the recess, he announced that he would prorogue parliament within days of its return in early September until 14 October.[29]

Combined with Johnson's insistence that he would happily take the UK out of the EU without securing a deal with Brussels, the threatened prorogation galvanised backbenchers. In a highly controversial move, opposition parties and Conservative rebels worked together to pass the European Union (Withdrawal) (No. 2) Act, a short piece of legislation introduced by the Labour MP Hilary Benn which was intended to prevent a no deal exit unless it had been explicitly authorised by parliament.

The Benn Act was not only controversial because it made unusual use of parliamentary procedures – using an emergency debate to provide the time for the bill to be discussed – but, more fundamentally, the passage of a law proposed by backbenchers without the consent of the government called into question the very nature of parliamentary sovereignty.[30] The government and its supporters took the view that the backbench bill was unconstitutional because it had been passed without the authority of ministers, by backbenchers who could not be held accountable for its effects. Some even suggested that the government should advise the Queen not to give her consent to the bill once it had passed. Others – including myself – argued that parliament was the ultimate authority and that if a majority of MPs and peers had approved the bill, then it was perfectly constitutional for it to become law.[31] Because Johnson did not have an independent majority in the Commons and his own party was split over Brexit, the bill's supporters managed to find the majorities they needed.

Boris Johnson saw the Benn Act as confirmation that the House of Commons was the main obstacle to his delivering Brexit and being re-elected Prime Minister. He decided to dial up his rhetoric, pitting the referendum mandate against parliamentary sovereignty accordingly. He repeatedly described the Benn Act as 'a surrender bill', saying it was 'designed to overturn the biggest democratic vote in our history' because it sought to prevent a 'no-deal' exit on 31 October. He argued that the MPs who had voted for it had committed 'a great dereliction of their democratic duty'.[32] The media was briefed by anonymous sources that he intended to break the law by refusing to ask the EU for an extension to negotiations, as the Benn Act required.

Once the Benn Act had been passed, Johnson tried to secure a general election in order to gain a workable majority in parliament – although he protested that another popular vote was the last thing he wanted. When MPs refused to vote for an early election, he pressed ahead with his promised prorogation. Exercising the prerogative power to prorogue parliament was an extreme means of neutralising parliamentary opposition to his plans – a prorogued parliament cannot fulfil any aspect of its normal role. When parliament 'adjourns' for a recess, committees can still meet if they wish to scrutinise government decisions, but during a prorogation they cannot. Nor can MPs or peers legislate, hold debates or ask questions of ministers.

The public statements made by MPs made it very clear that the House of Commons which returned from recess in September – ahead of the impending 31 October deadline – had plenty of appetite to do all these things. But documents considered by the Supreme Court demonstrated this was not a consideration for the government. An official memorandum sent to the Prime Minister on 15 August focused entirely on the benefits of prorogation for advancing the government's political goals, ignoring the question of what parliament itself might have wanted to do in the run up to the Brexit deadline.[33]

Johnson's decision to prorogue parliament and his accompanying rhetoric about the unimportance of parliament's absence at a crucial moment in the Brexit process was designed to justify the prorogation. His wider narrative about the illegitimacy of parliament's actions – before and after the attempted prorogation – was intended to support his case for a general election – which he calculated (correctly) would return him to power with a large enough majority to 'get Brexit done'. Some would say that this rhetoric was justified and necessary to overcome the parliamentary stasis which had been produced by the combination of Brexit and the hung parliament.[34] Conservative MP Robert Halfon argued that the prolonged hold-up was in itself 'undermining trust in democracy'.[35] But in achieving its political ends the government did considerable harm to public perceptions of parliament – delivering a hammer blow to the reputation of the legislature which it could ill afford.

And Boris Johnson's rhetoric did not only affect the public's view of parliament as an institution. His accusations that MPs were in dereliction of their democratic duties and 'surrendering' to the EU had serious consequences for public perceptions of MPs individually too. In the wake of the Supreme Court's judgment on prorogation, the Commons chamber saw some of the most acrimonious and vicious exchanges in living memory. The rhetoric of 'parliament versus the people' rose to fever pitch. Johnson maintained that 'The people of this country can see perfectly clearly what is going on. They know that parliament does not want to honour its promises to respect the referendum',[36] and lambasted what he called the 'zombie parliament' for holding the electorate hostage. His supporters chastised MPs for refusing either to support the Prime Minister or to grant him an election. 'This parliament is a dead parliament,' the Attorney General, Geoffrey Cox, declaimed before the Commons. 'It should no longer sit. It has no moral right to sit on these green benches ... This parliament is a disgrace.'[37]

The bombast may have been aimed at MPs, but his words resonated well beyond the Commons chamber. Online abuse of MPs – already at alarming levels – rose manifold in the hours and days after the debate. The *Financial Times* identified a 392 per cent increase in 'toxic' tweets compared with the average over the previous week. These came from both sides of the Brexit divide.[38] MPs on all sides of the debate reported that the volume of threats they received increased dramatically during the Brexit process. Some were forced to stop holding open surgeries on the advice of the police. In May 2019, a neo-Nazi was jailed for life for a plot to murder the Labour MP Rosie Cooper, while Luciana Berger MP saw six people convicted of threats to her and her family.[39] As I discuss in Chapter 2, this was not just an unpleasant period in the lives of MPs. For many it shaped their calculations about whether to stand again at the subsequent election, and thus the future make-up of the House of Commons.

The government restricted parliament's role on Covid-19

During the Brexit crisis it was argued that UK parliament was dealing with unprecedented and unique circumstances. But parliament had barely returned following the 2019 election when Westminster – along with the rest of the world – was hit by a second unprecedented event – a global pandemic. Just as Boris Johnson's 80-seat victory looked set to return the House of Commons to the business-as-usual of majority government, Covid-19 completely reset the government's priorities and necessitated radical and speedy reworking of parliament's practices and procedures.

The pandemic situation was undoubtedly novel, but the government's approach to parliament during the Covid-19 crisis had an unpleasantly familiar feel. Again, government chose to side-line parliament during a moment of national drama – minimising the importance of its contribution and unilaterally limiting its ability to fulfil its role – while pressing ahead with highly controversial policies which radically reshaped the lives of UK citizens. This time, the government's substantial majority meant that parliamentarians were powerless to resist being side-lined. While the small majority and minority governments of 2016–2019 put significant power in the hands of MPs, the situation was now reversed –

parliamentary dominance being replaced by executive dominance.[40]

One early government decision which decisively shifted the focus away from parliament, was to hold daily press conferences in Number Ten.[41] During previous national emergencies, it would have been normal for the Prime Minister and his senior ministers to make regular statements in the House of Commons and submit to questioning by MPs. During the pandemic, daily scrutiny was conducted instead by journalists and occasional carefully vetted members of the public. Whereas the journalists were in pursuit of a neat soundbite for the evening news, MPs questioning ministers would have been looking to elicit practical information on behalf of their constituents, to dig into inadequate responses with follow-up questions and ultimately to influence the government's policy. Holding press conferences made it much easier for the government to control public health messages – which was very important – but the press conferences also allowed it to evade detailed scrutiny of its response.

For MPs, the frustration of being unable to question the Prime Minister and his senior colleagues on a regular basis was increased by the difficulty of getting answers through other mechanisms. The early technical limitations of the 'hybrid parliament' in which MPs could participate either in person or online meant decisions had to be taken by the government and opposition front benches about what business to prioritise. Westminster hall, adjournment, opposition and backbench debates –all normally useful mechanisms for MPs to raise issues and elicit information from the government– were sacrificed to allow government business, including the passage of legislation required to deal with the pandemic, to proceed.

Parliamentary questions were also affected. Many went unanswered during the early months of the pandemic as some government departments struggled to cope. The Department of Health and Social Care (DHSC) (which even in normal times is the department which receives the most questions from MPs) was singled out for particular criticism by MPs.[42] This may be unsurprising given the pressure on the DHSC to mount the UK's response to Covid-19, but it left MPs unable to scrutinise that response or elicit vital information on behalf of their constituents.

Just as day-to-day scrutiny of government was limited during the pandemic, scrutiny of legislation was reduced to the bare minimum (as discussed in the introduction to this chapter). At the start of the pandemic, there was cross-party consensus on the need to give the Johnson government the powers it decided it needed to make secondary legislation to respond to the virus. The Coronavirus Act, which created many of these new powers, was passed following just a single day's scrutiny in the Commons and without votes – the need for physical 'divisions' – which were difficult with social distancing – having been avoided through inter-party negotiations.

But as the weeks and months passed, the opposition and government backbenchers became less and less sanguine about the use that government was making of its new powers, and others available to it in pre-existing legislation. According to analysis by the Hansard Society, by the end of August 2021 ministers had made 486 pieces of Covid-19-related secondary legislation, using powers conferred in 132 Acts of Parliament, 7 Orders, 5 EU Regulations (which had become retained EU law in the UK) and one Church Measure.[43] As it became clear that Covid-19 was going to affect the UK, and indeed the world, for years rather than months, disquiet grew among MPs and peers about the extent to which the government had used urgency procedures to bring in measures such as local lockdowns before they had been signed off by parliament. In some cases – MPs accepted – it was necessary for the government to act swiftly, but what Ruth Fox of the Hansard Society described as 'ministers' habitual use of 'urgent' powers'[44] meant that in most cases MPs were only able to conduct scrutiny retrospectively. This created a problem of accountability – as the academic Ronan Cormacain has argued: 'Relegating parliament to the subordinate role of merely rubberstamping legislation makes government unaccountable to parliament.'[45]

The lack of scrutiny also affected the clarity and quality of the regulations. As case numbers began to climb in the autumn of 2020 and ministers began to impose varying restrictions on different areas of England, the public became increasingly confused about what regulations applied where and to whom, what was guidance and what was actually illegal. Noting this confusion, Lord Thomas, the former Lord Chief Justice of England and Wales, called for greater parliamentary scrutiny, arguing that:

> when it is known that the measures will be independently and publicly scrutinised by parliament, experience has shown that generally the result is better thought-through provisions, a clearer distinction between what is law and what is guidance and a more cogent explanation of the justification for the measures in the light of the available alternatives.[46]

Greater parliamentary involvement might have allowed for clarification, endowed the unprecedented restrictions on daily life with greater legitimacy and built much-needed trust in the government's approach.

By the autumn of 2020, concern was growing in parliament about the limitations on parliamentary scrutiny imposed by the government's continued use of the urgency procedure – described by the barrister and academic Tom Hickman QC as 'abracadabra law-making'. [47] In September 2020, the government wanted to pass a motion to allow it to keep using the powers in the Coronavirus Act. MPs who were opposed to the extension of the powers were outraged at the brevity of the debate allowed on the motion: 'Ninety minutes is an utter, utter disgrace,' said the former chair of the Procedure Committee, Conservative MP Sir Charles Walker. 'It is actually disrespectful to this House, and it is disrespectful to colleagues.'

A group of over fifty MPs led by the chairs of the Conservative backbench 1922 committee and the Parliamentary Labour Party tabled an amendment to the motion which was designed to guarantee parliament a say over future regulations.[48] Much was made in the debate of the importance of parliamentary scrutiny and the rule of law, but the Commons Speaker did not allow a vote on the amendment because – had the amendment been made – it would have created legal uncertainty about the government's use of the powers. Nonetheless, Sir Lindsay Hoyle took the opportunity of the debate to register his displeasure with way the government had treated the House of Commons. 'The way in which the government have exercised their powers to make secondary legislation during this crisis has been totally unsatisfactory' he said:

> All too often, important statutory instruments have been published a matter of hours before they come into force, and some explanations why important measures have come into effect before they can be laid before this House have been unconvincing; this shows a total disregard for the House … I now look to the government to rebuild the trust with this House and not treat it with the contempt that they have shown.[49]

In the months that followed, there was little change in the government's approach. In the year after the Coronavirus Act became law, the Commons was allowed just five hours of debate on regulations made under the Act. The government continued to publish regulations at the last minute and schedule votes only long after they had come into force. Throughout the pandemic the government has been at pains to express its reluctance to restrict the liberties of the UK population, but its practices have reflected a habit or even arguably a preference for prioritising its own ease of action over the effective functioning of parliament.

What should change?

Parliament's role in the law-making process and policy scrutiny have been dramatically reduced during Brexit and the Covid-19 pandemic. To some extent this has been due to the unavoidable constraints on the operation of government, but it has also been a matter of political choice.[50]

The years in which government and parliament have grappled first with Brexit and then with Covid-19 have damaged the relationship between the two and diminished the public's trust in both. Parliament's inability to bring the Brexit process to a conclusion undermined its public reputation, but the damage was exacerbated by the May and Johnson governments' political strategy of pitting parliament against the people. Parliament was unable to fulfil its role as a discussion and brokering mechanism, helping government to understand and balance the interests of different groups and organisations. Instead, it simply became the forum for a zero-sum battle between political opponents set on different visions of Brexit. During the Covid-19 pandemic the government minimised the role of parliament beyond what the emergency demanded. Parliament was often unable to fulfil its role of scrutinising and legitimising government activity, and was side-lined in a way which has diminished its value in the eyes of the public.

Government actions and words over the Brexit and Covid-19 period have repeatedly demonstrated a fundamental misconception about parliamentary sovereignty – that it is identical to the will of the executive. In a nutshell, governments appear to believe that the executive is entitled to get its way in parliament in all circumstances. The confusion may be understandable – the norm in the UK has been to have majority governments with a high degree of party discipline, so politicians have become used to what parliament does being synonymous with what government wants. But this is an inaccurate reading of parliamentary sovereignty as meaning executive sovereignty.[51] This misconception needs to be challenged because – as I have shown – its consequences are damaging for government's relationship with parliament.

Government should change its approach to parliament for two reasons. First, in the public interest, because when parliament is allowed to do its job properly it enhances the processes and practices of government through debate, scrutiny and accountability. Second, out of self-interest, because strengthening parliament's reputation will ultimately strengthen the credibility and trustworthiness of government.

Ministers gain their mandate to govern from the parliament from which they are drawn, which means that – as the historian Robert Saunders has argued – 'A government that sets itself against parliament, or that refuses to obey its laws, shuts off the source of its own democratic authority.'[52] As the Supreme Court reminded us in its judgment on the second Miller case:

> We live in a representative democracy. The House of Commons exists because the people have elected its members. The government is not directly elected by the people (unlike the position in some other democracies). The government exists because it has the confidence of the House of Commons. It has no democratic legitimacy other than that.[53]

The public look to parliament to represent their interests and provide a check on government. If they think that parliament is not capable of doing these things effectively – in part because ministers treat it as unimportant – they will cease to value it. At the same time, the public will lose trust in ministers who appear to govern without checks and balances, setting up a downward spiral of trust and effectiveness.

Ministers must reset their approach to legislating, ensuring that parliament has the opportunity to debate and scrutinise fully formed policy proposals – rather than simply being asked to sign off ever greater powers for ministers. This means showing parliament more bills and regulations in draft and allowing sufficient time for and between stages of scrutiny. Learning from the frustrations and conflict of the Brexit years, the government should relinquish its iron grip on the agenda of the House of Commons – sharing responsibility for determining the House's business with opposition parties and backbenchers by creating a cross-party committee responsible for agreeing the House's business each week.

And ministers should schedule opportunities for back-benchers and the opposition to set the agenda regularly throughout every session – not restricting them when it does not suit ministers to be subject to scrutiny.

Public trust in the authority of parliament underpins the UK's entire system of government – no government should seek to undermine it for short-term political gain. Scrutiny should be welcomed as a means to improve laws, policies and their delivery. Accountability should be accepted as the corollary of executive freedoms. In the wake of the divisive Brexit years, ministers should recognise the value of parliament – not as a forum for conflict but as a mechanism for communicating with the public – for demonstrating that it is also possible for politicians to work together for the common good to find ways of balancing the problematic trade-offs which are inherent in the difficult business of governing the country. The government should overtly recognise the legitimacy of the roles which parliamentarians play and validate the efforts of MPs and peers to play those roles in a way which demonstrates they are worthy of public trust.

And, as I go on to discuss in Chapter 2, the government should support efforts to make parliamentarians themselves more diverse, so that all groups in society can have confidence that their interests are being represented in the corridors of power.

Unrepresentative

Introduction

'This is a wonderful place,' the Speaker John Bercow told the members packed into the Commons chamber, 'filled overwhelmingly by people who are motivated by their notion of the national interest, by their perception of the public good and by their duty – not as delegates, but as representatives – to do what they believe is right for our country.'[1]

Out of context, his statement reads as an uncontentious endorsement of the value of the House of Commons from an enthusiastic and loyal proponent of parliamentary democracy. But context is crucial: Bercow was speaking on 9 September 2019 – the day on which (as discussed in Chapter 1) the Prime Minister had announced he would close down parliament for five weeks, ahead of a new parliamentary session that would begin just days before the UK was due to leave the EU. Later that day, Boris Johnson would ask MPs to back a motion for an early general election – a vote he said he did not want, but had been forced to hold in order to break a parliamentary logjam and allow him to 'get Brexit done' in line with 'the will of the people'.

Greeted by an ovation and applause from rebel conservative MPs and many on the opposition benches, and by stony silence from most government members, the controversial Speaker's remarks were not simply an endorsement of his colleagues. They were a pointed reminder of what he saw as their duty as members of the House: to vote according to their conscience and their judgement of what was in the best interests of the UK – 'as representatives' of the people, rather than 'as delegates' reflecting the wishes of their constituents or following their party line.

Most MPs – including the Prime Minister – would agree with this articulation of the role of an MP – famously formulated by the eighteenth-century MP Edmund Burke. A YouGov survey of 100 MPs conducted in 2019 found that 80 per cent believed they had been elected 'to act according to their own judgement, even when this goes against the wishes of their constituents'.[2] What the Speaker and Prime Minister did not agree on was what was 'right for the country' in these circumstances. Bercow was opposed to the prorogation – which he went on to describe as 'an act of Executive fiat'.[3] He wanted MPs to vote as individuals rather than as members of particular parties, to stop parliament being closed down. Johnson wanted MPs to vote for an early election, to ensure he could deliver Brexit to his promised timetable, without interference from his parliamentary opponents. He was prepared to take a hard line against dissenters – the previous week he had thrown 21 MPs out of the Conservative party for supporting a rebel motion designed to prevent a 'no-deal' exit.

This vignette of the intense days at the start of September 2019 highlights the complexity of the representative role of an MP, who must balance their own views with those of their party, their conscience and their constituents. It also illustrates how Brexit forced the question of the myriad ways in which MPs might claim to represent their constituents on to the political agenda. In this chapter, I consider how the unrepresentative nature of MPs, in terms of their characteristics and backgrounds, contributes to a lack of public confidence that their interests are being represented in the House of Commons. I discuss how the Brexit process exacerbated voters' concerns about the role played by MPs, contributing to a downward spiral of public confidence in parliament, and discuss what could be done to improve the diversity of MPs and, in doing so, to help reverse the decline.

Representative or delegate?

In modern times, there has tended to be a high degree of alignment between the views of an MP, the party on whose manifesto they stood and the constituents who voted for that manifesto. There might be one or two issues on which an MP's views would diverge from those of their party – because of a strongly held personal position or a particular constituency concern – but in most cases members would expect to vote with their colleagues, following the guidance of the whips. A minister quoted in *The Times* in early 2019 articulated the previous strength of this norm: 'You don't get to pick and choose. You vote with your whip. That's it. That's what you're here for. Maybe once in a blue moon, perhaps once in your entire career, there is something you really cannot support, and you have a chat with the whips.'[4] This used to mean that a member of the public voting for an MP would be able to be reasonably confident that, once elected, they would support all the key elements of their party's manifesto.

In recent decades, however, the norm of strict party loyalty has begun to break down. According to Philip Cowley, an academic who has tracked the rebelliousness of MPs, 'One of the most striking developments in the House of Commons over the last 50 years has been the rise of backbench dissent. MPs are increasingly willing to vote against their party line.'[5]

Brexit significantly accelerated this trend, throwing expectations about how MPs should perform their role up in the air – because views on the UK's membership of the EU cut across traditional party-political lines. 'Nowadays it's just a free-for-all', complained the same minister quoted in *The Times*. A majority of MPs campaigned to remain in the EU and then found themselves having to deliver an outcome they had opposed. Most committed to honour the result of the referendum – fearing the corrosive impact on public trust of failing to do so – but they held a wide spectrum of views on the UK's future relationship with the EU. Numerous MPs found that their own judgement about the best outcome for the UK did not accord with the position of their party – some found they were at odds with the balance of opinion in their constituency. Many Remain-supporting MPs represented constituencies where a majority of people had voted to leave, but there were also 34 MPs holding the opposite position – including at the most extreme, vocal Brexiter Kate Hoey MP in 78 per cent Remain-voting Vauxhall.

These discrepancies generated heated debates in the media about whether MPs were failing to fulfil their responsibilities if they voted differently in parliament to the way their constituency had voted in the referendum.[6] What made it particularly hard for MPs was the May and Johnson governments' narrow or non-existent parliamentary majorities: a decision to rebel could have very real consequences for their party. Under a majority government, an MP can rebel and register their dissatisfaction with a government proposal without risking a government defeat. But under the minority governments of May and Johnson, government defeats were common – between 2017 and 2019 May suffered more defeats than any government since the 1970s.[7] The votes cast by individual MPs became the subject of media comment and were highly visible to the public. In November 2017, the *Daily Telegraph* ran a front page headlined 'The Brexit Mutineers' featuring pictures of 15 Conservative MPs who had rebelled against the government during the passage of its flagship EU Withdrawal Bill.[8] This and similar coverage incensed some members of the public: the Conservative MP Anna Soubry was just one of those who reported a sharp rise in the threatening abuse she received on social media following the publication of the article.

The concerns of voters about whether MPs were representing their views on Brexit in parliament are likely to have been exacerbated by another wider political trend – that of loosening voter allegiance to political parties.[9] During the Brexit period, researchers found that whether an individual had voted 'Leave' or 'Remain' in the referendum became a more important defining feature of identity than traditional party-political allegiances.[10] Even two years after the referendum, in 2018, only 6 per cent of people said they did not identify with either Leave or Remain, whereas 21.5 per cent said they had no party-political identity. For many, whether their position on Brexit was being represented in parliament became more significant than whether their wider political views were being reflected. Given the wide spectrum of public views on Brexit, any final deal could only meet the exact aspirations of relatively few.

As discussed in Chapter 1, the period between the EU referendum in 2016 and the UK's final departure from the EU at the end of 2020 was corrosive of public trust in MPs. Watching the House of Commons navigate the Brexit minefield exacerbated existing public dissatisfaction with MPs. The public has long differed from MPs in its view of how elected members should represent their constituents; unlike most MPs – a majority of the public think members are elected to act according to the wishes of their constituents, even when this goes against their own judgement. By 2019, the Hansard

Society's annual Audit of Political Engagement found that only 25 per cent of the public had confidence in MPs' handling of Brexit and 42 per cent agreed that 'the UK's problems could be dealt with more effectively if the government didn't have to worry so much about votes in parliament'.[11]

Substantive and descriptive representation

In relation to Brexit, what most voters cared about was whether MPs were acting in their interests – as they saw them – by voting for their personal preferred outcome from the process. In the academic literature this is known as 'substantive' representation – MPs shaping policies in the interests of those they represent.[12] Many academics who have investigated the subject see substantive representation as closely related to 'descriptive' representation – whether MPs mirror the characteristics and background of those they represent – and it is this aspect of MPs' role as representatives that I explore in this chapter.

It is obviously possible for MPs to represent people who are not like them. But it is intuitively persuasive that people with a range of different characteristics and backgrounds need to be present in decision-making bodies such as the House of Commons if their interests are to be fully represented.[13] This argument has been made most forcefully by feminist academics talking about the representation of women, but it can be extended beyond gender to other all the other aspects of identity that the public will recognise when judging whether the ranks of MPs embrace 'people like them'. This includes – but is not limited to – ethnicity, class, age, disability, gender identity and sexual orientation.

In respect of some of these aspects of identity, the characteristics of MPs as a group diverge noticeably from the wider population. It is therefore unsurprising that on some issues the views of MPs and those of the public also diverge. Brexit was one such issue: research shows that voting 'leave' was associated with older age, white ethnicity, low educational attainment, adverse health and low life satisfaction. Remain voters tended to be younger, more ethnically diverse and more educated. [14] Leave voters were justified in suspecting that many MPs did not agree with them on Brexit because their respective judgements were shaped by different characteristics and experience.

Are MPs representative of the UK population?

The simple answer to the question of whether MPs are (descriptively) representative of the UK population is 'no'. In general, the House has become more diverse over time. But in some respects – despite some concerted efforts in recent decades – progress remains painfully slow – MPs continue to diverge significantly from the population they represent. And the public is conscious of this – a YouGov poll conducted in 2019 found that fewer than one in five Britons believed MPs were representative of the UK population while less than a quarter (only 24 per cent) believed the House was getting more diverse.[15]

The difference in the numbers of male and female MPs is one of the most visible aspects of diversity on which the Commons falls down. The year 2018 marked the centenary of the law which made it possible for women to be elected to parliament,[16] but in the hundred years since 1918 we have failed to achieve parity in the representation of men and women in the House of Commons. In total, only 558 women have *ever* been elected to the Commons – nearly 100 fewer than the 650 MPs who sit in the House at any one time. Yes, there has been an upward trend – from just 19 female MPs elected in 1979 (3 per cent of the total) to 220 women elected in 2019 (34 per cent) – but this still leaves the UK languishing joint thirty-ninth in an international league table of women's representation in legislatures.

If numbers of women MPs continue to increase at the same rate as they did between 1979 and 2019, it will take another twenty years to achieve gender parity in the House of Commons (and slightly longer until women comprise the same 51 per cent of the House they do of the general population). But we cannot assume a continued trajectory towards parity of representation. The latest data from the Inter-Parliamentary Union (IPU) shows that while the global share of women in parliaments is slowly rising – reaching 24.9 per cent in 2020, up from 11.3 in 1995[17] – there have been setbacks. The 50 countries which held elections in 2018, for example, elected on average 25.8 per cent women MPs, which was less than the 27.1 per cent women elected in the 37 countries which held elections in 2017.

Between 1995 and 2020, 10 of the 172 countries for which the IPU collects data saw either no progress or a reduction in the proportion of women MPs.[18]

The House of Commons could easily see a similar reversal, not least because the female MPs currently in the House of Commons are not shared equally among parties. While over half of Labour's MPs are women, only a quarter of the Conservative parliamentary party is female. A particularly poor general election result for Labour could slash the number of female MPs, unless the Conservative party does more to redress the imbalance among its own candidates.

The Labour Party only reached gender parity by taking dramatic steps to ensure women could stand in winnable seats. In 1993, Labour began using all-women shortlists – a form of gender quota – to improve the representation of women in the Commons. According to the IPU, 'Quotas have been a key determinant of progress in women's political participation. Of the top twenty countries with the largest share of women in parliament in 2020, sixteen apply some type of gender quota.' In 1996, an industrial tribunal ruled all-women shortlists unlawful in the UK on the grounds of sex discrimination, but Labour had already used them to select candidates in thirty-eight 'winnable' seats to be contested at the 1997 election. The women selected won in thirty-five of the seats, bringing the total number of Labour MPs to 101. This had a transformative effect on female representation in the Commons – doubling the number of women MPs from 60 to 120. In 2002, Labour passed the Sex Discrimination (Election Candidates) Act legalising all-women shortlists. The party has continued to use all-women shortlists in the two decades since, with considerable success, culminating in 2019 in 51 per cent of Labour MPs elected being female.[19]

At the behest of David Cameron after he became Conservative Party leader in December 2005, the Conservative Party took measures designed to make his party more appealing to voters, including by increasing the number of female and minority ethnic Conservative MPs, peers and MEPs on a so-called 'A-list'. Names on the A-list – over half of whom were women – were recommended directly to constituency parties electing candidates to stand in top target seats, and put forward in the handful of seats which held open primaries to choose candidates in the run-up to the 2010 general election.[20] In 2010, Helen Grant became the first black woman to be elected to represent the Conservative Party (among a total of 11 Conservative and 15 Labour minority ethnic MPs). But the overall impact of these measures has been relatively underwhelming: of the Conservative MPs elected in 2019, less than 25 per cent are women and only 6 per cent are of a minority ethnic background.[21]

What about forms of diversity other than gender?[22] People identifying as having a disability are significantly under-represented in the House of Commons too: just five current MPs declare a disability. Although it is likely that more current MPs have invisible disabilities they have not chosen to discuss in public,[23] the House of Commons still lags way behind the 20 per cent of the population who consider themselves to have a disability.[24]

In terms of ethnicity and sexuality, the 2019 election delivered the most diverse House ever. Sixty-five MPs from non-white ethnic backgrounds were returned – making up 10 per cent of the total number in the House. This was the largest number since 1987 when the first group of four MPs were elected who were not white. This contrasts with the situation even as recently as 2005, when only fifteen – just one in forty MPs elected – were from a minority ethnic background.

Nonetheless, there would need to be another twenty-eight additional minority ethnic MPs to reflect the composition of the UK population, in which 14.4 per cent are minority ethnic. At the same rate of progress as between 1987 and 2019 (and again a smooth trajectory cannot be taken for granted), it will take another thirteen years for the Commons to be representative in terms of ethnicity. It is also notable that the ethnically diverse MPs who have been elected are not spread evenly across the UK: there are no black, Asian or other minority ethnic MPs at all from Scotland, Wales or Northern Ireland. Based on the make-up of the devolved nations, a representative House of Commons would include at least three Scottish and two Welsh MPs from a minority ethnic background.[25]

Following the 2019 election, *Pink News* described the UK parliament as 'the gayest in the world' on the basis that – according to unofficial data – at least forty-five MPs had been elected who were 'out' as lesbian, gay, bisexual, trans or as having another minority sexual orientation or gender identity.[26] There may, again, be other members who have chosen not to disclose this aspect of their identity. But based on these figures, and estimates about the UK population, individuals with a minority sexual orientation or gender identity are currently under-represented by about thirty-eight MPs;[27] an openly transgender person has never been elected to the UK parliament.

MPs are generally older than the general population; the median age of an MP has remained static at around 50 since 1979, compared to a population average of 40. There has been a slight upward trend, as there has in the average age of the UK population. Between 1979 and 1997 most MPs were in the age bracket 40–49, but every election since then has returned most MPs in the age bracket 50–59. At the 2019 election, the average age of MPs elected was 51, with the youngest – the 'Baby of the House' Nadia Whittome MP – aged 23, and the oldest – Bill Cash MP – aged 80.[28] Members at either end of the age spectrum – aged under 29 and over 70 – each represent just 3 per cent of the total number of MPs.[29]

The education of MPs can be loosely used as a surrogate for their class background, and analysis of where today's members went to school and university reveals another respect in which they are unrepresentative of their constituents. Of the MPs elected at the 2019 General Election, 29 per cent attended fee-paying schools (compared to 7 per cent of the wider population[30]), 88 per cent were graduates (compared to 42 per cent of adults in the labour market[31]) and 21 per cent attended the universities of Oxford or Cambridge (compared to 1 per cent of graduates). Looked at by party, Conservative MPs elected in 2019 were the most likely to have attended a fee-paying school: 41 per cent compared to 30 per cent Liberal Democrat, 14 per cent Labour and 7 per cent SNP, according to the Sutton Trust.[32]

Why does diversity matter?

So, MPs are more male, straight and able-bodied, less ethnically diverse, older and more likely to have had a privileged education than the UK population they represent. But does this lack of diversity matter, and if so, why?

The Equality and Human Rights Commission argues that 'Diversity of representation is important for the democratic principles of equality, effectiveness, fairness, justice and legitimacy.'[33] Similarly, the Speaker's Conference on Parliamentary Representation – an investigatory commission set up by the Commons to look at the disparity between the representation of women, ethnic minorities and disabled people in the House of Commons and in the UK population – argued that

> While justice is the primary case for widening parlia-mentary representation, there would also be real benefits for both parliament and wider society if the House of Commons were to be made more fully representative ... in addition to justice ... We believe that a more representative House of Commons would be a more effective and legitimate legislature.[34]

The first reason why the House of Commons should be diverse, then, is a matter of basic justice – that it should be equally possible for anyone in the UK who wants to become an MP (and is eligible to do so) to stand for parliament. If there are structural or societal barriers to standing for election for groups of people with certain characteristics, then that is unfair and unjust. The Speaker's conference argued that these impediments – including time, cost, culture, support and confidence – could be considerable, but such barriers may not be apparent to members of the public.

Second, there is a symbolic case for a more diverse House of Commons. It is damaging to the credibility of parliament – the institution which passes laws on equality, diversity and inclusion for everyone in the country – not to exemplify these qualities itself. This is not just a problem of inconsistency. Inevitably, the gap between what MPs decide for the rest of the country and what they (literally) embody themselves determines their authority in setting the rules. Consequently, a lack of diversity in the House of Commons itself is likely to reduce the efficacy of the laws and regulations it passes. As the academic Sarah Childs has argued, the House of Commons ought to aspire to 'embody the principle of equality and fairness, acting as a 'role-model' institution'.[35]

The third case for diversity is 'effectiveness' – that a legislature works more successfully, especially on behalf of minority groups, when those groups are better represented. Both academic and observational evidence suggest that this is true: who is represented in a legislature affects what it achieves for different groups, and under-represented groups may suffer.

The academics Rosie Campbell, Sarah Childs and Joni Lovenduski analysed data from two mass surveys (the British Election Study and the British Representation Study series) on attitudes to gender and representation among voters and elected representatives. They found that male representatives were, on average, not as hostile to traditional gender roles as women voters. The academics argued that this meant male representatives might be less likely than female representatives to act on gender-related issues on behalf of women voters. They also found that, although female voters were more supportive than male voters of increasing the presence of women in decision-making bodies like the House of Commons, this support declined across the generations (with the youngest women being least enthusiastic). The academics concluded that 'while women may not want more women representatives, they continue to need them'.[36]

Although it is quite possible for MPs who have not had a particular experience to tackle it on behalf of their constituents, circumstantial evidence indicates that they are more likely to be aware of and therefore to raise issues of which they themselves have experience. The Labour MP Harriet Harman has argued that it was only when she and other female MPs entered the House of Commons in sufficient numbers in the 1980s that issues such as childcare and domestic violence began to advance on to the political agenda.[37] The Fawcett Society has also highlighted how social issues such as the minimum wage and sex discrimination became more prominent after the proportion of women in the House increased in 1997.[38] There is a sizeable global literature which illustrates a relationship between the presence of women in legislatures and their consideration of issues affecting women.[39]

Having a more diverse range of MPs makes it more likely that a wider range of issues affecting under-represented groups will be raised. Recent notable examples of MPs drawing on their own personal experience include contributions in debates on parental bereavement,[40] mental health[41] and racism.[42] When such issues are marginal or stigmatised in society, the value of their being openly discussed in parliament can be considerable, and an MP's contribution to the debate may have a greater impact if it draws on their own experience.

A more diverse parliament may also be more effective because of how it operates. As I discuss later in this chapter, an institution founded by one group of people – in the case of the House of Commons older, privately educated, white men – will inevitably reflect the habits and ways of operating preferred by that group. When one group dominates there is a risk that their practices – which may not suit other groups of people – are assumed to be the only way that politics can and should be conducted. This can create a powerful blocker to reform. The Speaker's Conference reported that MPs had found 'that the culture, style and attitude of the House of Commons has begun to shift towards being less confrontational and aggressive since more women were elected'.[43] But female MPs continue to report the style of debate in the Commons chamber being a barrier to their participation. And as anyone watching the House of Commons debate Brexit in the autumn of 2019 would have concluded, it is easy to reverse apparent progress in building a more inclusive style of politics.

The fourth reason why increasing the diversity of the House of Commons is important is because, for those groups in society who are less well represented, the legislature may seem less legitimate. Even though most MPs will do their best to represent all the issues and experiences faced by all their constituents, it is inevitably easier for them to overlook the concerns of groups of which they are not a part and to neglect the significance of experiences which they have not had. Members of under-represented groups, seeing decisions that will affect their lives being made by people who are not like them, who perhaps seem to neglect their perspective, may feel less inclined to see those decisions as valid. The Covid-19 pandemic has shown that public distrust of government decisions can potentially have life-threatening consequences. Among certain minority ethnic groups, distrust of vaccines has reduced take-up among some of those most at risk from the virus. While there may be multiple reasons for such 'vaccine hesitancy', research by the University of Wolverhampton found that minority ethnic respondents reported mistrust of government – including concerns about their community being used as 'guinea pigs' for trials to verify vaccine results.[44]

Back in 2010, the Speaker's Conference noted that, among the public, there was 'a widespread perception that MPs, and parliament itself, are divorced from reality', arguing 'There is little sense that Members understand, or share, the life experiences of their constituents.' Since then, efforts to make parliamentary business more topical and relevant have reduced the perception that parliamentary debates bear little relation to the most pressing issues of the day. The introduction of 'topical questions' to ministers – which can be asked on any subject without notice – and the creation of an online public petitions system, have improved the degree of correspondence between a day's newspaper headlines and the subjects under discussion in the Commons. But while the topics under discussion may be closer to key issues of public concern, there is little evidence that the public think the people debating them have a greater understanding of their own point of view. If sections of the public do not respect the people taking decisions in the House of Commons, that is damaging for it as an institution and our democratic system more broadly.

Who wants to increase diversity?

Despite these various arguments for greater diversity in parliament, the public is not convinced. In an experimental study in 2012, Rosie Campbell and Philip Cowley investigated how the personal characteristics of hypothetical MP candidates affected whether study-participants would vote for them. It found that voters' assessments of candidates were more affected by the prospective MPs' acquired characteristics – education, occupation or where they lived – than by their gender or age.[45] Religion was also less significant. This study was echoed by a 2019 YouGov poll in which three in five respondents said that gender or gender identity, ethnicity, religion and sexual orientation were not important when selecting prospective MPs (62, 59, 68 and 68 per cent, respectively).[46] The same survey found that a significant chunk of the public – around two-fifths – were opposed to measures to improve the diversity of candidates, including all-women shortlists, gender quotas or lists of preferred ethnic minority candidates. Public preferences are not in themselves a reason not to adopt such measures – there are many past examples of politicians introducing progressive policies 'ahead' of public opinion – but low public appetite may reduce the incentive for politicians to champion such policies.

In contrast to the public, all the UK's main political parties have accepted the premise that the Westminster parliament should be more diverse and have made varying efforts to increase the diversity of their candidates (as discussed above). These efforts have been very much in line with international consensus on the importance of increasing parliamentary diversity. Many other countries have adopted measures designed to accelerate improvements in diversity, and with some success. In November 2020, for example, New Zealand elected 'one of the most diverse parliaments in the world' – almost half-female, 11 per cent LGBTQ, and with people of indigenous Māori and Pacific Island heritage represented at a slightly higher rate than in the wider population.[47] This diversity was then reflected in the new cabinet of Prime Minister Jacinda Ardern. The UK is signatory to a number of international agreements which include a focus on achieving gender parity in political representation, including the 1995 'Beijing Declaration and Platform for Action', the 2030 Agenda for Sustainable Development (which established the Sustainable Development Goals) and various UN and Commonwealth declarations.

Like the UK's political parties, MPs collectively have begun to take the diversity of their own institution more seriously. Shortly after convening the 2008–10 Speaker's Conference on Parliamentary Representation,[48] mentioned above, MPs passed the Equality Act 2010, making it unlawful to discriminate, harass or victimise individuals because of their 'protected characteristics', and containing measures to encourage political parties to tackle under-representation, promote diversity in elected offices and increase participation in the democratic process.[49] However, a decade on from the passage of the Act, the section which requires political parties to publish information on the diversity of candidates (106) has still not been brought into force. The commencement of Section 106 – a vital step in understanding and increasing the diversity of the pipeline of people wanting to become MPs – has been part of the campaign by the Centenary Action Group established to mark the 2018 anniversaries of women's suffrage.

Some MPs have continued to take up the issue of representation. In 2014, a report by the All-Party Parliamentary Group on Women in Parliament titled *Improving Parliament: creating a better and more representative House* examined the barriers and challenges to recruiting and retaining women in public life.[50] The following year, the academic Sarah Childs published *The Good Parliament* – a 'blueprint for a more representative and inclusive House of Commons' – a practical analysis based on a year of study embedded in the Commons. The former Speaker, John Bercow, took up Childs's central recommendation that he establish a 'Reference Group' with a remit to drive forward change, but his successor Sir Lindsay Hoyle did not re-establish the group when he took over in 2019.

Why is diversity increasing so slowly?

Changing the make-up of the House of Commons has been a slow task. Under the current laws and with existing party practices, opportunities to make changes in the composition of the Commons are infrequent. We may have had three elections in the four years between 2015 and 2019, but in more 'normal' times an opportunity to alter the composition of the House comes only every five years (aside from an occasional by-election). Add to this the advantage of incumbency, which means that, having been successful once, an MP is more likely to retain their seat than to succumb to a successful challenge, and the possibilities for turnover are fewer still.

The pipeline of potential candidates who could stand for election is shaped by a number of 'push' factors, including structural inequalities entrenched in society. Disparities in opportunities and resources may inhibit potential candidates from under-represented groups from standing. Disabled people and individuals from minority ethnic communities are more likely to have been disadvantaged by discrimination or to be living on low incomes and unable to manage the upfront costs of standing for election, while women are more likely to have caring responsibilities which would make the itinerant, unpredictable life of an MP difficult to contemplate. These inequalities in society mean that the pool of would-be MPs starts off less diverse than the UK population. But the difficulty of changing society to deliver a broader pool of candidates simply strengthens the case for changing the practices of politics to accommodate a wider range of people.

The selection practices of the main political parties – who usually win the majority of seats in the UK's first-past-the-post system – have the potential to both exacerbate and redress the situation. In reality – as Labour's successful use of all-women shortlists demonstrates – an additional 105 female, 28 minority ethnic and 38 LGBTQ MPs could readily be brought into the House of Commons across just a couple of general elections. But only with the political will to do so.

With party membership in the UK on the decline, prospective parliamentary candidates are often chosen by a small group of party activists – in some cases just a couple of hundred. This means that the decisions of these small groups of party members are crucial in determining the diversity of the individuals who stand a chance of election. These 'selectorates' have particular power in 'safe seats' which have been held by the same party for decades. In the 2019 general election, 30 per cent of Westminster seats (192) had not been held by a different party since before 1945 or even earlier. This meant that nearly fourteen million potential voters effectively had their MP chosen for them by members of the party which held the monopoly in their area: the views of the electorate on the merits of the various candidates, including their personal characteristics, were largely irrelevant. This is why measures such as all-women shortlists are potentially so influential and also so controversial: because they work.

Addressing the 'pull' factors that would persuade the widest possible diversity of candidates to stand for election and enable them to function effectively in the House when they arrived, has been slow work too. It has proven difficult to persuade existing MPs to make changes to the way it is run that might make it more inclusive and encourage more diverse candidates to stand. As Sarah Childs noted in *The Good Parliament*, 'the House remains unrepresentative, and its working practices continue to reflect the traditions and preferences of Members who have historically populated it'. The members currently populating the House are a self-selected group who accepted its shortcomings when deciding to stand for election. On arriving in Westminster for the first time, MPs may be surprised or dismayed by its practices, but most quickly become inured to the inconveniences of the role, and few devote much time to considering the wider effect of these factors on other potential candidates.

Never has the limiting effect of incumbent MPs on potential innovation been more in evidence than during the Covid-19 pandemic. The crisis compelled legislatures around the world to adapt and reinvent their procedures to allow their members to keep fulfilling their roles. The Commons and the Lords innovated rapidly. The need for social distancing shrank the capacity of the Commons chamber from over 400 to just 50 – preventing many MPs who were shielding, isolating, caring for dependants or unable to travel because of government restrictions from participating. But within weeks, from a standing start, the Commons and the Lords were equipped with systems for remote voting, arrangements for online committee meetings and hybrid chambers furnished with large screens to allow members to participate either online or in person at the same time.

Many of these innovations had significant benefits in terms of inclusion. Select committee members could participate in meetings from wherever they happened to be, and isolating members could still participate in votes. But unfortunately, these innovations – which would have had the potential to shift the dial on the diversity of MPs – have not been allowed to outlast the exigencies of the pandemic.

Analysis by the House of Commons Library found that female MPs were more likely than their male colleagues to participate remotely in hybrid proceedings, and more likely to certify as eligible to use a proxy vote at least once.[51] The Library observes that female MPs may have found it harder to be physically present in parliament during the pandemic because they took on a larger share of the caring responsibilities imposed by the pandemic than their male colleagues, in line with women in the wider population.[52] If the possibility of being able to vote remotely and participate in chamber proceedings online had been retained – at least for exceptional circumstances – it might have encouraged some people who would not otherwise have contemplated a career as an MP to have done so. People with caring responsibilities or disabilities that would make frequent travel difficult might have considered standing for election. But the decisions on whether to retain these innovations were not for them. Nor, in most cases, were they for MPs collectively – the government discontinued the new practices by simply letting them lapse – without providing an opportunity for a vote.

What should change?

There is much that could be done by the political parties to increase the supply and demand for diverse parliamentary candidates. But there is also much that MPs themselves could – and should – do to create a House of Commons that is representative of the country. MPs need to give greater priority to making the House of Commons a more attractive destination for diverse candidates and to enabling those who are elected to operate effectively once they arrive – so that they wish to stay. This would increase the effectiveness of the Commons and improve its credibility with the public, helping to reverse the vicious cycle of declining confidence which has been exacerbated by Brexit.

Progress has been made in recent years. Former Speaker, John Bercow, was the driving force behind the establishment of a nursery – making it easier for those with children to juggle their jobs and parental responsibilities – and was the first to allow MPs to take their children into division lobbies and to breastfeed in the chamber. A pilot of proxy voting for MPs on baby leave – allowing one MP to cast a vote on behalf of another – was finally introduced after the Labour MP Tulip Siddiq delayed her caesarean to participate in a crucial Brexit vote in January 2019,[53] and made permanent in September 2020.[54] Meanwhile, the establishment of a permanent select committee on Women and Equalities has signalled MPs' growing recognition of the importance of issues of equality and diversity.

But much remains to be done. The Commons needs to become more inclusive for those who visit and work there – in terms of its physical environment, its culture and the way it operates.[55]

The Palace of Westminster is an iconic, historic building which has great symbolic value to the nation. It is appropriate that the national legislature should be housed in a building with physical gravitas – Westminster has that in spades – but it can also be intimidating and warren-like – particularly to those on the outside looking in. And it is not only the physical characteristics of the building that can make people feel excluded, but also the unspoken rules which govern the use of its spaces. The Labour MP Anna McMorrin – asked what surprised her about the job of an MP when she was first elected – described 'The archaic nature of it all with some crazy rules such as staircases and chairs that only Members can use and that there are at least four times the number of men's rooms than for women.'[56] The parliamentary estate may lend grandeur, but it undermines any perception of parliament as a modern workplace.

Most of the 'crazy rules' which govern the physical use of space on the parliamentary estate have historic origins, and some continue to have a strong justification (such as ensuring MPs can get to the chamber in time to vote), but their cumulative effect can be to be off-putting. Even after having worked in the palace for over a decade, I still found it quite possible to wander into spaces in which I felt unwelcome and conscious that I might be admonished for inadvertently breaking some unwritten rule.

Young, female and minority ethnic MPs continue to complain about occasions when they have been profiled and challenged inappropriately. Experiences like that of the black Labour MP Dawn Butler, who was physically removed from the Members' Tearoom by a member of security staff, even though he had been told she was an MP, led to the redesign of the security passes worn by everyone on the estate. But problems persist. Abena Oppong-Asare, a Labour MP newly elected in 2019, tweeted about a series of incidents in which she was confused with other black MPs or assumed to be a member of staff. In a survey conducted by ITV news in early 2020, 62 per cent of the 37 black and minority ethnic MPs who responded said they had experienced racism on the House of Commons estate and 51 per cent said they had experienced racism or racial profiling from fellow MPs.[57] The larger the numbers of diverse MPs who get elected to the Commons, the easier it will be to challenge assumptions (among MPs themselves as well as the wider public) about who belongs in parliament, but that does not make the negative experiences of current MPs any more acceptable.

Practical steps should be taken to address the disparity in the provision of facilities for men and women on the parliamentary estate, as well as to ensure that the Commons is accessible to MPs and members of the public with different physical requirements. In *The Good Parliament* Sarah Childs identifies glaring problems – like the difficulty for MPs who use wheelchairs of joining their colleagues on the front and back benches – which, she argues, might be addressed by refashioning the Commons chamber. The lack of office space near the chamber for MPs with mobility difficulties could also be addressed by reorganising existing functions. Improved audio provision would make life easier for MPs with hearing impairments, and parents of both genders would benefit from greater provision of baby changing, feeding and caring facilities across the estate. As someone who has changed their child on the floor of a parliamentary toilet and breastfed in the corner of a deserted committee room, I heartily agree. Childs argues for more accessible toilets designated on the assumption of future parity of gender representation among MPs and for unisex or gender-neutral facilities. And she suggests that, to make the palace less foreboding for constituents, witnesses and other occasional visitors, more informal meeting spaces should be created, similar to those in the atrium of Portcullis House.

The planned restoration of the Palace of Westminster represents a golden opportunity to address the accessibility of the Victorian palace, and – while both Houses move out into alternative accommodation – to experiment with alternative ways of working. But efforts to make the House of Commons a more inclusive space should not wait for the 'restoration and renewal' project, which, as I discuss in Chapter 5, may take decades to complete or indeed never materialise.

Alongside the need to change the fabric of the House of Commons there are issues of culture which affect who aspires to become an MP. One factor which undoubtedly affects the diversity of the House of Commons is the confrontational nature of its proceedings. While passionate debate may be a desirable feature of politics, the House of Commons is often singled out among other legislatures as having a particularly adversarial atmosphere. In part this stems from the first-past-the-post electoral system which has tended to reward two main political parties, setting up an antagonistic culture. This is reinforced by the physical set-up of the chamber in which the government and opposition parties face each other across a central aisle from parallel benches. Although the arrangement of the chamber originated in the mid-sixteenth century when the Commons began sitting in the opposing benches of St Stephen's chapel, subsequent opportunities to move to the more collegiate 'in-the-round' setting preferred by most other parliaments have been forgone,[58] illustrating Winston Churchill's maxim that 'we shape our buildings and afterwards our buildings shape us'.

The UK's electoral system and the set-up of the chamber undoubtedly contribute to an oppositional politics. But building a hemicycle and ending first-past-the-post would not necessarily dismantle this culture, as the creation of the Scottish parliament has demonstrated.[59] Neither, on the other hand, is it inevitable that Westminster's characteristics should lead to confrontational parliamentary proceedings characterised by aggressive, sexist and exclusionary language. The frequency with which these occur in Westminster is down to choices made by politicians, the tendency of the media to focus on the most high-octane exchanges and nostalgic narratives designed to defend this particular way of 'doing' politics.[60]

This culture has real consequences for MPs, as demonstrated in the autumn of 2019 when the House of Commons was dealing with the Brexit 'endgame'. As discussed in Chapter 1, angry debates and personal attacks in the chamber were picked up and magnified on social media. David Gauke MP, one of the Conservative MPs who had been thrown out of the party for voting against a 'no-deal' Brexit, said he was 'worried about the use of language ... It is incredibly divisive, it is designed to stoke resentment, provoke anger, to nurse grievances, and it is feeding into a toxic atmosphere, not just in parliament but I think more widely.'[61]

Many other MPs, including former ministers Amber Rudd, Dominic Grieve and Justine Greening and Labour MP Paula Sheriff, noted the connection between extreme language used in the Commons and the numerous threats they received. The June 2016 murder of the Labour MP Jo Cox, by a man inspired by right-wing nationalist rhetoric, loomed large in the minds of all concerned.

This was not just an unpleasant period in their lives of MPs. For many it shaped their calculations about whether to stand again for election in 2019. While the impact was not just on women, it did seem to have a disproportionate effect on the decisions made by female MPs. Announcing her decision not to put herself forward again for election, Conservative MP Nicky Morgan cited 'the clear impact on my family and the other sacrifices involved in, and the abuse for, doing the job of a modern MP'. Heidi Allen, a former Conservative MP who had moved to the Liberal Democrats, alluded to 'the nastiness and intimidation that has become commonplace' as one reason she had decided to stand down.

What should give us particular pause is the number of younger female MPs who decided in 2019 that they could no longer subject themselves and their families to the unpleasantness and risk that holding public office involves. While the number of female MPs who gave up their seats was in proportion to the gender balance of the House of Commons, most of the male MPs who stood down did so after a long career in politics. By contrast, many of the women who chose to leave the Commons did so after only a relatively short time in office.

And the impact may not only have been on existing MPs. Who knows how many eminently qualified individuals may have been dissuaded from standing for parliament by the toxic exchanges in the Commons and the vitriol directed at MPs on social media?[62] The parliamentary candidates who gave evidence to an inquiry by the Committee on Standards in Public Life in 2017 overwhelmingly agreed that intimidation was discouraging individuals from standing for public offices.[63] And the Committee found that intimidation was disproportionately likely to be directed towards parliamentary candidates who were women, from ethnic and religious minorities, or LGBTQ.

There is an obvious connection between the culture of the House of Commons and the attitude of the public towards politicians – an aggressive style of politics legitimates hostile attitudes towards MPs on mainstream and social media. The abuse which this engenders is having an impact on the diversity and quality of our politicians. 'We are operating in an incredibly nasty, hostile, Twitter-fuelled environment,' a senior, male backbencher told me. 'People are frightened a lot of the time.' The exposure of our elected representatives to such pressures is worrying. We will be left with an even less diverse and representative set of MPs if we reach a situation where only the most thick-skinned or self-sacrificing are willing to put themselves forward for election.[64]

There is nothing inevitable about the composition of the House of Commons. The make-up of the Commons today is the result of a history of exclusions of different groups in society, from the formal (for example legal restrictions on who could stand for election) to the informal (including physical environment and culture).

It matters that the House of Commons is not representative of the UK population. An unrepresentative House is only unjust in principle but impairs its effectiveness and undermines its credibility and legitimacy in the eyes of the public. It is in MPs' own interests to take action, as well as those of potential future MPs and the constituents they would represent. But at the moment, the leadership that would be required to bring this change appears to be absent. Much of the responsibility lies with political parties, but MPs themselves also need to take responsibility for changing their institution, including by addressing the incomprehensibility of parliamentary proceedings – as I discuss in Chapter 3.

Arcane

Introduction

In Westminster, 19 October 2019 was a bright autumn day. The patch of grass opposite the House of Lords that houses the temporary media 'village' that springs up to cover momentous parliamentary events was lined with fluttering EU and Union flags, decked with placards and patrolled by vocal protesters with megaphones. This was 'Super Saturday' – the first time the House of Commons had met on a weekend since the Falklands conflict, and the day – the government hoped – it would finally persuade MPs to back its Brexit deal.

Depending on how you counted, this was the fourth, perhaps the fifth time the May and then Johnson governments had tried to win a so-called 'meaningful vote' in the Commons – a precondition insisted on by parliament before it would pass the law required to take the UK out of the EU. Following the failed prorogation and the House of Commons' refusal to give Boris Johnson the general election he wanted, the clock was ticking down to the 31 October deadline agreed with the EU as an extension to the Article 50 process.

The government had tabled a motion approving of Johnson's deal – which it needed MPs to support to keep its hopes of the UK leaving on 31 October alive. That was because backbenchers who were opposed to the idea of a 'no-deal' Brexit had managed to pass a law – the Benn Act – saying that the Prime Minister would have to ask the EU for an extension to the Article 50 process if he had not got the Commons to endorse either a deal or 'no deal' by 19 October. Johnson had sworn he would rather 'die in a ditch' than contemplate asking for an extension.

By the time Super Saturday arrived, MPs opposed to 'no deal' had conceived a new worry – that MPs who actively wanted the UK to leave without a deal might support the meaningful vote – neutralising the Benn Act – but then refuse to vote for the law needed to give effect to the deal. Without that legislation on the statute book the UK would, by default, leave without a deal. To avoid this possibility, Conservative backbencher Oliver Letwin had proposed a change to the government's motion. His amendment withheld MPs' approval for the deal until after the necessary legislation had been passed.

At 2.30 p.m., after a fractious morning of debate, MPs backed the Letwin amendment by 322 votes to 306.

So far, so clear. But what happened next was the subject of considerable confusion. After the amendment passed, the government decided not to trigger a vote on the 'main question' (whether MPs agreed with the government's original motion – now amended by Letwin). Instead, it allowed it to pass without a 'division'.

This provoked an outcry among some MPs. They took to the airwaves bemoaning the government's decision to 'pull' the meaningful vote they had been expecting, and journalists picked up and repeated their complaints. As the academics Meg Russell and Lisa James wrote subsequently: 'A combination of unreliable briefings and limited procedural knowledge … risks drawing journalists unwittingly into spreading misleading information.'[1] Some MPs were upset because they had wanted to vote for the deal, others because they wanted to demonstrate their opposition to it. A few – including the Democratic Unionist Party – wanted a deal but were opposed to the so-called 'Northern Ireland Protocol'; others wanted to reject any deal and leave without one; still others wanted a different deal or the opportunity for a 'People's Vote' before agreeing any deal.

But all of those who criticised the government for not holding the vote were mistaken. Why? Because the reason I relate these events is not to give you flashbacks to the torrid days of autumn 2019 – when parliament became the epicentre of the country's Brexit divisions. Rather it is to illustrate that, amid all the sound and fury, a good number of members had not grasped a simple aspect of how the House of Commons works – the process of voting on a motion. Their anger at the government was misplaced because once the Letwin amendment had been passed it was impossible for them to have the vote they wanted.

One MP who did understand what had happened – the Conservative backbencher Steve Baker – had to explain the logic on BBC *Newsnight* that evening: 'I know it's incomprehensible,' he said, correcting the misunderstanding of the presenter Emily Maitlis about what had happened, 'and I'm sorry for journalists having to report this stuff; it is a little bit complicated.'[2] As he explained, once the Commons had agreed to the Letwin amendment, the motion that the government had originally tabled – asking the Commons to agree with its deal – no longer existed. The Letwin amendment had removed most of the original words in the government motion and replaced them with the words 'this House has considered the matter but withholds approval unless and until implementing legislation is passed'. It was on these amended words that the government declined to have a vote. Once the amendment had been made, the government knew that the amended motion would pass, so there was really no point in pushing the question to a vote. Having forced its MPs to be in Westminster on a Saturday, the government was keen to let them return to their constituencies rather than spend another twenty minutes pointlessly trooping through the division lobbies.

To those who have not worked in parliament, this description of Commons processes probably does sound 'a little bit complicated'. Like Emily Maitlis, even specialised political journalists assigned to cover the story were struggling to be sure they had understood it correctly. As the journalist Raphael Behr observed of parliament's Brexit machinations more broadly: 'For onlookers it has been an impenetrable struggle.'[3] But it is worrying that there were actual members of parliament who did not understand what had gone on.

Worrying, but understandable. Because the way the House of Commons works is complicated. Too complicated. Having evolved over hundreds of years, parliamentary rules have become nearly impossible for the general public to understand, hard for the media to grasp and – most alarmingly – difficult for MPs themselves to comprehend – creating disparities in the ability of MPs to do their job. In my view this is fundamentally undemocratic. It is no wonder that public trust in the House of Commons has continued to spiral downwards, and it will likely continue to do so unless MPs make efforts to transform their private club into a public House.

The public cannot understand the House of Commons

It is inevitable that parliamentary rules will have some complexity – MPs need to be able to do a range of different things to fulfil their roles of conducting scrutiny, holding debates and passing legislation. But the complexity of House of Commons procedure goes well beyond what is necessary to allow members to do their jobs. This is a problem because it prevents the public understanding what is done in their name. There are three reasons why this matters, in particular for those who want to change government policy or the law.

First, complex procedures and jargon-filled language make it difficult for the public to understand what is going on in their parliament. If an MP said, 'Today I went to the Table Office and signed an Early Day Motion, intervened in an Adjournment Debate and tabled amendments for the Report stage of the Agriculture Bill', how many of their constituents would have any idea what they had been doing all day? When news broke in August 2019 that Boris Johnson had decided to 'prorogue' parliament, almost no one could have told you that this meant that almost all parliamentary business would be formally suspended until parliament was reopened by the Queen and a new parliamentary year began.

Another good example of difficulties with parliamentary language is the convention of MPs referring to each other in the chamber by their constituency rather than their name. This convention was established before the days of radio and television to help maintain courteous exchanges by reminding members that they are speaking on behalf of their constituents. But today it makes the simple question of who is talking to whom during a parliamentary debate unanswerable for the vast majority of spectators. MPs often highlight the importance of this convention in 'taking the heat out of' a debate which might otherwise become personalised. But unfortunately, this may be more of an indictment of the aggressive nature of UK politics than an argument for retaining a convention which is a significant barrier to public understanding of parliament.

If the public do not understand what MPs are doing it makes it less likely that they will value their work and the House of Commons as an institution. The public could be forgiven for seeing the complex rules of the Commons as governing an exclusive, political game – particularly given that even some MPs see them that way. As a former minister told me, 'For some members procedure is part of the game of politics; a tool to score points from your opponent in the Oxford Union or the sixth-form common room'. Worse, the public may suspect that the complexity of the rules is actually intended to prevent the public understanding what is going on in the private club of Westminster.

The second reason that the complexity of Commons rules and the jargon-filled language which surrounds it matter is because they encourage the media to portray parliament's procedures as malfunctioning. Sometimes journalists can be too ready to accept the spin MPs put on events in the House of Commons – in particular their tendency to blame procedure rather than acknowledge their own failures (as discussed at the start of this chapter). On 30 September 2020, for example, the *Guardian* reported on a backbench attempt to give the House of Commons a bigger role in decisions on Covid-19 regulations (mentioned in Chapter 1). 'An overwhelming number of backbench MPs had publicly backed an amendment to grant them more say,' the paper reported, 'though that was thwarted by parliamentary procedure.' The impression created by the article was that procedure had been an impediment to the working of the Commons. This perception was understandable, but wrong. The Speaker – Sir Lindsay Hoyle – had applied the rules as normal. The MPs backing the amendment had hoped that that he would interpret the rules in a way that departed from precedent and allow them to amend a statutory motion. But the way the story was reported made it seem as if it was the rules of the House of Commons themselves that were the problem.

On other occasions, journalists prefer to gloss over the details of rules they find hard to understand or poke fun at procedures they find hard to explain to their audience. This is problematic because it encourages the public to see the House of Commons as the butt of a joke rather than an important part of the process. There is undoubtedly a market for stories about 'men in tights' and arcane procedures dating from the seventeenth century. Some members of the public find the historical mystique of parliament as alluring as many MPs. But I would bet that most citizens would be willing to exchange that nostalgia for the confidence that they were being run by a modern, competent parliament which they could easily understand. Nor are a sense of history and a comprehensible legislature mutually exclusive. It would be quite possible to retain some of the ceremony, formality and associated flummery which are characteristic of the House of Commons while radically improving the accessibility of its procedures.

Enthusiasts for the EU now regret the effect that trivialised reporting of its activities (including alleged restrictions on 'bendy bananas'[4] and excessively powerful vacuum cleaners) may have had on the reputation of Europe in the UK. There is a risk that by making light of the contribution made by our parliament, lampooning the complexity of its rules and highlighting the archaism of some of its procedures, the media may contribute towards the public distrusting and undervaluing it, just as they did the EU.

The third reason that it is problematic is that the public cannot understand the rules of the House of Commons is that it means there is an uneven playing field for those wishing to amend the law or even understand how changes to legislation happen. The complexity of the rules governing law-making are one reason for the existence of a thriving industry of lobbyists who advise their clients on how to influence those laws – a profession which came under the spotlight in 2021, first following revelations about David Cameron's lobbying on behalf of the collapsed finance firm Greensill Capital and again when former Conservative minister Owen Paterson was found guilty of taking payment for lobbying on behalf of two private companies.[5] Those organisations who can afford the advice of public affairs professionals have the best chance of spotting opportunities for changing new laws in ways which would be advantageous to them.

When I worked in the Commons' legislation office it was easy to see the access which it is possible to buy. The job of clerks in the Public Bill Office (PBO) is to advise MPs on the amendments that they might want to suggest to bills as they make their way through the Commons.

Some MPs come to the PBO with a vague idea of something they would like to achieve but no idea how to go about it. In that case it is the job of the clerk to draft amendments on behalf of the MP.[6] Some MPs will have a go at drafting their own amendments. The official opposition and other party spokespeople will have some support from party staff to do this. When they bring their proposed amendments into the office, the clerk's job is to check them for sense and 'orderliness' – making sure they do not contravene any parliamentary rules – for example ensuring they are within the 'scope' of the bill they want to change.[7]

The third variety of amendments which you see as a PBO clerk are the ones suggested to MPs by organisations with an interest in the legislation. These might be charities, businesses, trade unions or trade associations. Amendments of this type usually appear at 'committee stage' when there is the greatest chance of their being debated and made lobbyists will work out which MPs are on a bill committee and who is likely to be sympathetic to their client's point of view and send them lists of possible amendments. These are recognisable because they arrive in the PBO as pre-printed lists, normally competently drafted with legal support.

To be clear, there is nothing wrong with an MP proposing amendments that have been drafted by other organisations – assuming they have not accepted any inducement to do so and personally agree with the objectives of the changes they are suggesting. But because the legislative process is very difficult for the public to understand and engage with, individuals or organisations who can afford to pay can get the great advantage of advice on how to achieve what they want. There is an uneven playing field because the rules of the game are not equally accessible to all.

Some attempts have been made to open up the law-making process to the public. Public evidence sessions are now held on most bills, during which their main provisions are discussed with invited experts. Occasionally 'draft' bills go through an extra process of 'pre-legislative scrutiny' where a committee takes evidence and recommends changes before the bill is introduced into the House. And select committees occasionally choose to hold inquiries into proposed new laws which relate to their area of interest. But none of these innovations do anything to help the public understand the law-making process itself.

What is procedure?

To really appreciate the complexity of Commons procedure, you need to understand where the rules are set out. The short answer is – in lots of places. Just like the UK's infamous 'unwritten' constitution, much of the Commons rule book is written down, but it is not 'codified' – set out helpfully all in one place.

The core of the Commons rules is the Standing Orders – decisions of the House about how to run itself – which are periodically published in little blue books (also available online). I say 'little', but the latest print version runs to 200 pages. Most of the individual Standing Orders are permanent, but others are time-limited – used when MPs want to trial a new procedure, or do something for a fixed term. Recent examples include a temporary standing order passed to allow a pilot of proxy-voting for baby leave[8] and another establishing a committee to scrutinise the Brexit negotiations. The rules change quite often, which means if you are looking something up, it is important to be sure you are looking at the most up-to-date edition of the Standing Orders.

Asked where to find the rules of the House of Commons, many MPs would reply 'Erskine May'.[9] This weighty tome – a 'treatise on the law, privileges, proceedings and usage of parliament', often referred to as 'the bible of parliamentary procedure' – was first produced in 1844 by the parliamentary librarian (later chief Clerk) Thomas Erskine May. Now in its twenty-fifth edition, Erskine May is not really a rule book at all but an account of the way that the procedures of the Commons (and the Lords) have evolved over time and the conventions that govern them. If you want a really comprehensive picture of that evolution, you need not only the most recent edition of May, but also all the previous editions to see how procedures have got to where they are today.

The importance of Erskine May is that it not only sets out the decisions the House has taken about how to run itself, but also includes the conventions (otherwise unwritten rules) that affect how everything works. One good example is the Salisbury Convention, which dictates that the House of Lords will not vote down a government bill which was mentioned in the government's election manifesto – ensuring that even without a majority in the Lords, every government should be able to keep its key legislative promises. There are numerous other conventions governing what happens in parliament, from what MPs should say in their maiden speech, to how MPs should refer to each other in the House. MPs need to be aware of many of these conventions to function effectively in the House of Commons – particularly in the chamber.

Erskine May also documents important precedents – examples of what has been done in the past. As with common law, these precedents are influential (although not conclusive) in determining what should happen in future, including by establishing what should not happen (documenting instances when things have gone wrong, or decisions have been made that are considered 'bad precedents'). For example, precedent governs the question of the 'casting vote' – that is how the MP who is in the chair should cast their vote if a division in the House or a committee is tied. This became relevant in the House of Commons chamber (for the first time in 26 years) in April 2019 when the Commons was voting on whether to hold more 'indicative votes' on alternative Brexit outcomes. When the vote on this question was tied – with 310 MPs voting for and 310 voting against – the Speaker John Bercow cast his vote with the 'noes', following the precedents which dictated that – as it was not possible for him to vote in a way that would prolong the debate – he had to vote 'no' to avoid creating a majority where none had existed before.

Following the precedents on this occasion was a choice. It was open to the Speaker to act against previous precedents, as he did in January 2019 when he controversially decided to allow the Conservative MP Dominic

Grieve to amend a 'business motion' setting out the timetable for debate on Theresa May's Brexit deal – something that previously would not have been allowed.[10] Bercow justified his decision on the basis that it allowed the House to take a decision it wanted to take – it being an important duty of the Speaker to interpret 'the will of the House' and try to facilitate it. He argued that it would be wrong for previous precedents to prevent this happening, noting that 'If we were guided only by precedent, manifestly nothing in our procedures would ever change.'[11]

It is difficult to disagree with that observation, although, at the time, opinions on its relevance to the decision in question diverged strongly. But the fact that Bercow decided to dispense with previous precedent illustrates my point: to operate effectively in the House of Commons, MPs need to understand the conventions and precedents which guide its procedures, as well as the rules which are written down. And even when they may think they understand those unwritten rules, it is still possible for them to change. One reason for the existence of the Speaker is to have a final arbiter of the rules to interpret how they should apply in any new situation – but during the 2017–19 parliament John Bercow's novel interpretations of procedural conventions and standing orders introduced numerous uncertainties.

Erskine May is a pretty good guide to rules, precedents and conventions. But until the most recent edition was published – the 25th in 2019 – it was only available in hard copy. Its price tag of hundreds of pounds meant only the most committed (and wealthy) proceduralists had one on their bookshelf. Happily, after a lengthy campaign to '#FreeErskineMay', the text is now also available online.[12] This means that MPs need not fork out for a copy and – if need be – can even consult it on a tablet or smartphone while in the chamber.

Moving Erskine May online should mean that it is more reliably up to date. Rather than having to wait for ten years for the emergence of a new edition – a time period somewhat longer than the 'week in politics' during which a lot can change – the online edition can, in theory, be more regularly updated. I say 'in theory', because despite the numerous procedural innovations that took place during the final phase of Brexit, amendments to the 2019 edition were not made until December 2021. This may be because many of the procedural precedents set during the Brexit period were still regarded as controversial or because the staff who were responsible for recording the necessary updates were busy dealing with the procedural implications of Covid-19, but it did mean a lot of new developments remained unrecorded for several years.

But even though Erskine May is now much more accessible, that does not mean it is easy to use. As one of those responsible for compiling the index of the 24th edition, I can attest to the fact that – even for parliamentary practitioners – it is not always obvious where to find what you want as you leaf through its exhaustively detailed pages. The language is complex and full of parliamentary jargon. The chances of any but the most experienced MPs being able to refer to Erskine

May for last-minute procedural guidance, while sitting in the Chamber, are slim to non-existent.

It is in recognition of this fact that the Commons authorities have established a Procedural Centre of Excellence – a small unit staffed with officials whose job it is increase the confidence and expertise of MPs in dealing with procedure. They have also produced the *MPs' guide to procedure* – a set of online and hard-copy resources designed to explain the most important and frequently used aspects of Commons procedure to MPs and their staff in plain English.[13] These efforts to explain the rules governing the things that MPs most commonly want to do are a great step forward, and build on procedural guidance previously offered to (although rarely taken up by) new MPs as part of their induction when they first arrive in the House. But they do nothing to address the enormous complexity of the rules themselves.

One might think that complexity is an inherent feature of the way that parliaments function. It is true that there are a large number of different activities or 'parliamentary proceedings' in which MPs participate, for which rules need to be set out. But the degree of complexity in the Commons' rules is not inevitable. It is the result of the accretion of centuries of decisions, and a system which is much better at adding extra provisions to address new circumstances, than culling unnecessary material in order to prioritise the clarity and usability of the rules. In 2015, for example, no fewer than 34 pages of new rules were added to describe the new 'English Votes for English Laws' procedure (known as EVEL) – designed to ensure that laws that affect only England, or England and Wales, are approved by a majority of English, or English and Welsh MPs.[14]

We can see that complexity is not an inherent feature of parliamentary procedure because the UK has three very good examples of other legislatures whose rules – formulated over recent decades rather than centuries – are very much more straightforwardly written than those of the House of Commons. And yet those parliaments function perfectly effectively. So do the various parliamentary assemblies of multinational bodies such as the Council of Europe, whose rules of procedure were drafted relatively recently.

The purpose of having rules governing parliamentary proceedings is to establish a clear, shared understanding of how things are supposed to be done, so that a parliament can carry out its business in an orderly manner which is fair to everyone participating. A secondary but important goal should be to ensure that the electorate can – if it wishes – understand the rules of the institution which governs them. If these are the goals, then the shorter, clearer and more user-friendly the rules, the more likely they are to be achieved. And if that is true, then other parliaments with simpler rule books are likely to be functioning more effectively than Westminster.

To anyone who has worked in Westminster it is obvious that the first goal I have suggested – of establishing a shared understanding of procedure among MPs – is not being achieved. There are significant disparities in the extent to which MPs understand and can therefore make use of the rules which govern the House of

Commons. A few MPs take pleasure in being 'procedural geeks', but even experienced members admit that they do not have a full grasp of the rules – the Conservative MP Sir Charles Walker told me, 'I ran the Procedure Committee for seven and a half years, but I know very little about procedure. I used to say, "I just drive the car, I'm not the engineer, the clerks know what's going on under the hood."' Most MPs are incurious about the procedures they are expected to follow and rely on party whips to advise them.

The reality of the gap in procedural understanding between different members is on display every time an MP is criticised in the media, or by their colleagues, for using an 'obscure' or 'archaic' procedure. Often, these MPs are simply making creative use of a totally normal procedure. Or sometimes they are relying on a rule which other MPs had not realised was in common usage. The Brexit process threw up numerous examples of such uses of procedure. For example, the Labour opposition deployed a longstanding procedure in a novel way when they used a 'Humble Address' motion to force the government to publish confidential papers relating to the Brexit process – much to ministers' outrage.[15]

The Speaker John Bercow drew on a normal rule of which many MPs were unaware when he told Theresa May that she could not bring her Brexit deal back to the Commons for repeated votes, because a question 'which is the same, in substance, as a question which has been decided during a session may not be brought forward again during that same session'.[16] Justifying his decision, Bercow noted that this was a rule that had been in operation since 1604. This prompted media coverage suggesting that he was relying on an 'archaic parliamentary rule',[17] which completely missed the point that although the rule *dated* from 1604, it has remained in daily use ever since. The 'same question' rule is important because it restrains ministers from trying to browbeat MPs into agreeing to a proposition. It is one reason why governments prefer to 'pull' votes where a rebellion is threatened – rather than risk losing and then being unable to ask the same question again in the same parliamentary year. The fact that the government did not anticipate the ruling and that some MPs appeared not to understand it illustrates again the impact that the complexity of the Commons rules can have on its proceedings.[18]

This situation seems wrong. Surely it is not desirable for the procedures of the Commons to be so complex that it is *possible* for procedural rabbits to be pulled out of hats by those who have gone out of their way to hunt them down? The energy required to do so could surely be better spent actually scrutinising government or acting on behalf of constituents. And would it not be preferable for all MPs to be operating on the same level procedural playing field? At the moment, some MPs – the ones who have been around long enough, asked enough questions or employed the most procedurally proficient parliamentary assistants – are better able to operate in Westminster and hence more likely to be effective on behalf of their constituents than the rest. This does not seem fair to those represented by newer or less well-informed MPs.

A confused MP should not look to their party whips for help with understanding what is going on. It is not in the interests of the whips to help their members understand procedure – the more an MP learns about the way the House of Commons works, the more likely he or she is to be able to come up with clever ways of achieving their own objectives, rather than those of their party. So it suits the whips for MPs to remain in the dark about exactly what is going on each day.

MPs do have support when it comes to understanding parliamentary procedure. The House of Commons employs hundreds of staff, including the clerks whose job it is to advise the Speaker, run committees, guide MPs on parliamentary questions and assist those who want to amend legislation as it passes through the House. The journalist Mark D'Arcy has observed that senior clerks perform 'a highly specialised role for which [they] have trained for decades'.[19] The fact that staff take years to develop an understanding of procedure demonstrates the difficulty for MPs freshly arriving in the House. But if they are to benefit from the knowledge and experience of clerks, MPs have to take the time and be prepared to ask for advice – and not all are willing to do so.

Why is procedure so complicated?

It would be wrong to imply that procedure never changes for the better. It is constantly evolving – with new precedents set, rulings made and innovations introduced.

Although the general trend is towards more rules and greater complexity, some changes have made procedure simpler and easier to understand. For example, clarifications have been made to parliamentary language, including the long-overdue decision in 2004 to refer to 'members of the public' rather than using the oddly derogatory term 'strangers', and the shift in 2006 from describing committees scrutinising bills using the perplexing term 'Standing Committees' to the more obvious 'Public Bill Committee'.

There have also been more radical improvements. Sir Charles Walker MP, the former chair of the Commons Procedure Committee, told me one of the most obvious had been the revitalisation of the public petitions process. By the twenty-first century, the original paper-based process of petitioning the Commons – which dated from 1669 – had practically fallen into disuse. In July 2015, the obscure, paper-based system was augmented by an accessible new website jointly owned by parliament and government.[20] 'It's really straightforward now,' Walker told me, 'the public can raise a concern, and have it debated – and everyone can get their heads around the 100,000-signature threshold for a debate.' Public engagement with petitions has grown exponentially. Petitions on subjects ranging from road pricing to Donald Trump have attracted millions of signatures and shaped the agenda of the House of Commons, if not always securing the change they wanted.[21] The most popular petition to date – calling for the UK government to revoke its request to leave the EU under Article 50

– received over 6.1 million signatures, although it obviously did not change the government's position.

The modernisation of the petitions process has been an example of a move in the right direction, but Commons procedure is not being simplified anything like quickly and comprehensively enough.

One reason why is that there is no one who has an incentive to highlight the issue of procedural complexity and hence no widespread acknowledgement that it is a problem. When MPs first arrive in the House of Commons, they are suddenly confronted with a super-complex set of rules, but at the same time by a host of other challenges that they need to address. They will be aware that longer-standing MPs have a better understanding of procedure and that – like with any exclusive club – gaining a working knowledge of the rules is part of the process of being accepted as a member. In these circumstances making a fuss about the difficulty of this task and highlighting their lack of knowledge is an unattractive proposition. Later, when MPs have been in the House for longer and might be expected to have learnt the rules, admitting to any lack of understanding is an even more unwelcome idea, especially when their prospects of continued employment are – at least in part – dependent on their ability to demonstrate their competence and effectiveness to their constituents. And when they have plenty of other priorities to fill their time, addressing the complexity of procedure is low on most MPs' 'to-do' lists – they have a strong inclination to think, 'if it ain't broke, why fix it?'

Nor is it likely that the initiative for radical reform of procedure will come from the staff of the House of Commons. Conservatism with a small 'c' is an essential feature of the way clerks do their jobs. In order to preserve their impartiality – which is crucial to enable MPs from all parties to work with them with confidence – they will hold back from offering opinions or venturing advice unless it is explicitly requested. The importance of this approach – intended to avoid any perception that staff might be pursuing an agenda of their own – was highlighted in January 2019 when the *Sun* newspaper splashed the headline 'Fury as senior Commons official "secretly plots with Tory rebels to derail Brexit"'.[22] In fact what the journalist had stumbled across was the normal process of a senior clerk providing advice to a backbench MP.

Some clerks are very reform-minded, and recent efforts to improve MPs' understanding of procedure are welcome. But the conservative approach of clerks means they are unlikely to propose radical changes to Commons procedure themselves, without MPs taking the initiative. They also have a further incentive not to initiate reform themselves. While clerks would benefit from MPs having a better understanding of procedure, this would also dilute the status that the 'high priests' of the Commons derive from their expertise.[23] Historically, the role of clerks as procedural experts has given them access to and standing with MPs and enabled them to keep control of many of the most senior management positions in the House of Commons administration (never mind that an intimate knowledge of Erskine May does not guarantee an individual will be good at managing people and budgets).

Another reason that procedural reform is slow is because of the nature of the mechanisms available to achieve it. One of the main mechanisms for review and innovation is the Procedure Committee – the group of MPs whose job it is to 'consider the practice and procedure of the House'. The committee is often the origin of sensible proposals for improving the procedure of the Commons, including ideas to simplify and modernise the rules.

One example is the Procedure Committee's 2016 proposals to reform the rules for Private Members' Bills (PMBs) – which are ideas for new laws proposed by backbenchers. Very few members of the public will have any idea that there are three different mechanisms for introducing a PMB, but that the opportunity to do so is governed not by merit or by the extent of parliamentary support for a bill, but by chance, stamina or party patronage. And the chances of any PMB becoming law are slim – a recent study estimated that on average only 5 per cent reached the statute book.[24] What many members of the public might suppose to be a genuine opportunity for backbenchers to legislate is, in reality, an elaborate and fictive procedure. In practice most MPs who introduce a Private Members' Bill do so not because they genuinely think it will become law, but in order to have the opportunity to make a speech in the chamber and tell their constituents that they are doing something useful. It is in the interests of most MPs to maintain this fiction. A senior backbencher told me, 'I've just had a lot of emails asking me to support Caroline Lucas's Ten-Minute Rule Bill. Do I reply to them and say – "there's no point, it's never going to become law?" No, I say, "I am watching its progress carefully."'

The Procedure Committee argued that the whole PMB process was 'misleading and opaque' to the public,[25] and came up with a package of sensible suggestions to reform it, but no government since has allowed the House the opportunity to take them up. It is not in the interests of the government to make the procedure for backbench bills work better, as this might distract from the government's legislative programme or allow backbenchers to take the credit for passing popular and effective laws.

This illustrates the Procedure Committee's key disadvantage – its limited powers.[26] Like any other select committee, the Procedure Committee can make recommendations to which the government has committed to respond within 60 days. But, also like any other select committee, it has no power to ensure that its recommendations are debated, much less implemented. All too often, unless there is some advantage to it in the recommendations, the government simply sits on Procedure Committee reports and provides no opportunity for the House to debate or agree to them. Thus, the vested interests of the governing party deprive the House of the opportunity to reform itself. Sometimes this happens in collusion with the Official Opposition, who often resist attempts to strengthen the role of backbenchers in anticipation of their own next period in power.

Periodically, the House of Commons has made more intensive efforts to modernise its procedures and make them more explicable to the public. A 'Modernisation Committee' was established under the Labour governments between 1997 and 2010, although the fact that it was chaired by a government minister – the Leader of the House – ensured it did not recommend anything that did not meet with government approval. In 2009, in an attempt to bolster the reputation of the House of Commons in the wake of the MPs' expenses scandal, Prime Minister Gordon Brown established the Reform of the House of Commons Committee (known informally as the Wright Committee after its Chair, Tony Wright MP). This made a series of suggestions designed to give the House greater control over its own activities, many of which were taken up by the incoming Coalition government in 2010, although some – most notably the idea of introducing a cross-party committee to agree the Commons' daily agenda – were dropped. A majority government can easily prevent the House of Commons implementing reforms that might be beneficial to MPs and the public, but which are not in the interests of the executive.

More recently, John Bercow arrived as Speaker with a modernising agenda. As discussed in Chapter 2, he made steps towards improving working conditions for parents. He reduced some of the traditional pomp and circumstance surrounding the Speaker's role – doing away with the gown worn by his predecessors, for example – although he actively cultivated other aspects of hierarchy within the system. Bercow encouraged procedural reforms that connected the House with the public and put significant emphasis on parliamentary outreach. After a false start he succeeded in his attempt to change the governance of the House of Commons by splitting the role of Clerk to create a Chief Executive – responsible for the running of the House – alongside the Clerk – the chief procedural adviser to the Speaker. However, even a Speaker who sought to actively pursue reform quickly ran up against the limits of his own role and the numerous roadblocks thrown up by the complex governance of the House of Commons – of which more later.

What should change?

MPs need to recognise that the complexity of their procedures is problematic and initiate processes to review and simplify them. How can this be done? Analogies with the UK legal system are helpful. The UK government has created mechanisms to modernise, consolidate and reduce the complexity of the country's legal system. Since 1965, the Law Commission has kept the law of England and Wales under review and recommends reforms where they are needed. Its aim is to ensure that the law is fair, modern, simple and cost-effective. With a more circumscribed but nonetheless daunting remit, the Tax Law Rewrite Project set up by HM Revenue and Customs was a major effort to rewrite the entire tax legislation of the UK in a way that was more consistent and understandable, replacing the archaic language and impenetrable terminology used in tax law with clear, modern vocabulary.

Following a similar model, the House of Commons needs to establish permanent mechanisms to review and rewrite its procedures – to reduce their complexity and modernise their language. These mechanisms should draw on extensive public engagement and receive support from experts on language and accessibility. The Commons Procedure Committee should oversee the process and make regular recommendations to the House on areas for reform.

But as I noted above, this will not be enough to secure change because the government can exercise a veto over the recommendations of the Procedure Committee.[27] This should change. Most select committees make recommendations about areas of government policy, and it is right that the government decides whether to take them forward. But the recommendations made by the Procedure Committee are about how the House of Commons runs itself. It ought to be for the Commons, not the government, to decide whether to implement them. The Procedure Committee needs the power to hold regular debates and votes on its recommendations – at least twice a year – without relying on the government to provide time. And although it will be impossible to prevent MPs being made aware of their party's preferences on any reforms, such votes ought not to be whipped. It should be up to MPs as individuals to decide how the House of Commons should be run.

In this way, we might start to make the strides we need towards the simplification and democratisation of House of Commons procedure. Because the task of levelling the procedural playing field for MPs and enabling the public to understand – and therefore value – what goes on in their parliament, is an urgent one. The perception that the House of Commons is a private club, run according to incomprehensible rules which set MPs apart from their constituents, persistently undermines public trust – a problem that I explore in more detail in Chapter 4.

4

Exceptionalist

Introduction

At 5.03 p.m. on Tuesday 23 June 2020, Jacob Rees-Mogg MP rose reluctantly to the dispatch box. Dressed immaculately as ever in a slightly oversized, double-breasted suit, the Leader of the House of Commons, often dubbed 'The Honourable Member for the Eighteenth Century' for his anachronistic, upper-class mannerisms, addressed the handful of MPs present in the chamber. 'This is a dreadful position for us to be in as a House,' he told them.

> The behaviour of a small number of Members of Parliament over years and decades has disgraced and shamed our parliamentary democracy, of which I, and many honourable Members, are so proud. Our ancient right that we should look after our own affairs is to be sacrificed, because the importance of restoring the trust of the British people in our system makes that the right thing to do.[1]

In comparison to the high-octane Brexit debates which had transfixed the country over the previous four years, the one-hour debate which took place on that warm early-summer evening was a little-noticed event. But current and former staff of the House of Commons were glued to the proceedings. Because the decision the House was about to take was the culmination of a two-and-a-half-year campaign to reform the way the House of Commons dealt with incidents of bullying and harassment.

The objective of the campaign had been to get MPs to recognise the principle which Rees-Mogg had just articulated – that MPs should not have the right to determine whether their colleagues had bullied others in parliament and how they should be sanctioned. The campaigners argued that people employed in the House of Commons should have the same right to properly independent HR processes as other workers across the UK. Over the decades, the rights of other employees had been protected by laws relating to equality, negligence and health and safety – but MPs had kept tight control of these processes. Party whips, who had a vested interest in suppressing scandal, were normally the final arbiters of the outcome of opaque systems in which staff had little confidence.

However much they might want or intend to, the campaigners said, MPs could never extricate themselves from the personal relationships and political considerations that would shape a decision on whether to reprimand, suspend or even expel a fellow member of the House of Commons. Former employment law barrister and Conservative MP Laura Farris highlighted the problem during the debate: 'any form of process which invites members to speak up for colleagues against a background of party allegiance and personal loyalties is fundamentally problematic'.[2]

Even as they watched the short debate that evening, the campaigners were far from certain that they would win. After two QC-led inquiries in the Commons (and a third looking at the House of Lords), numerous administrative initiatives, meetings and working groups, the House was being asked to agree the final crucial element of the system. This was the establishment of an Independent Expert Panel (IEP) which would take over the last two aspects of the process which still involved MPs – hearing appeals and deciding on sanctions. Up until this point these had been responsibility of the Committee on Standards – made up of seven MPs and seven lay members.

The House of Commons Commission – the small body of MPs chaired by the Speaker that is legally responsible for running the House – had conducted a consultation on the proposals for the IEP. The vast majority of those who responded to the consultation had argued that it was essential to remove the role of the Committee on Standards if complainants were to believe the new independent process was fair. On the other hand, most respondents agreed that if the IEP decided an MP should be suspended or expelled for misconduct then it was appropriate for the House to ratify that decision with a final vote. Democratically, a punishment that would temporarily or permanently deprive constituents of their elected representative should be taken by the House of Commons as a whole.

But – an overwhelming majority of respondents argued – the House should not be able to have a debate before the vote took place. The weight of opinion was clear. But there was to be a final twist in the story.

Despite the unequivocal findings of the Commission's consultation, the motion that the government put to the House said that MPs *should be able* to debate the decision of the IEP for up to an hour, not just to vote on it. Jacob Rees-Mogg argued that MPs had a 'constitutional right' to debate the most serious sanctions, allowing a 'short factual exposition of the process' rather than just signing them off.[3]

Staff – and the MPs who supported them – were aghast. Just as it had seemed that they were to get a properly independent process, the government had reinserted an opportunity for members to have the final word. There would be nothing to prevent an MP who had been found guilty from participating in the debate, while the person they had bullied – unless they were another MP – would have to sit and listen in silence. Past experience demonstrated that some MPs would feel no compunction in using such a debate as an opportunity to rehearse their defence.[4]

What was worse, from the point of view of complainants, were reports that, instead of allowing a free vote on the motion – as would be normal for a debate about the internal working of the House of Commons – the government had decided – highly unusually – to whip its MPs to support Rees-Mogg's proposals.[5]

Ahead of the June debate, the former High Court judge Dame Laura Cox, who had conducted the first inquiry into bullying and harassment of Commons staff, aired her concerns that allowing MPs to debate sanctions would have a 'chilling effect' and deter complainants from reporting cases.[6] During the debate, a number of MPs expressed the same worry. 'I really do have concerns about a bully pulpit being used in this Chamber,' said the Labour MP Meg Hillier. 'Even if people are not named, there will be gossip and innuendo about who is being referred to.' Others challenged the Leader of the House's assertion that their constitutional rights were under threat. 'The delegation of such decisions has no bearing on our sovereignty, whether we debate the matter or not', argued the Conservative MP Sir Bernard Jenkin.

In response to such concerns, the Chair of the Standards Committee, Labour MP Chris Bryant, tabled an amendment to the government's motion providing for IEP decisions to be voted on without debate. Remarkably, the government lost the vote on that amendment, despite its 80-seat majority – suffering its first Commons defeat following the 2019 election. MPs agreed by a five-vote majority that they should not debate the decisions of the IEP. The battle for a truly independent process had been won.[7]

MPs are special ...

The story of the fight for an independent bullying investigation process illustrates a persistent problem which undermines the reputation of the House of Commons – the tendency of MPs to treat themselves as an exception to the rules which they dictate for the rest of the country. This problematic assumption was again vividly illustrated in 2021, when the Johnson government attempted to change the Commons' standards rules rather than vote to sanction former Conservative minister Owen Paterson MP for paid lobbying.

In some important respects MPs *are* different to the rest of us – and for good reason. First and foremost, they are the elected representatives of the people and accountable to the people for their actions. As Conservative MP Edward Leigh put it as he argued against giving the IEP the right to determine sanctions against bullying MPs, 'The fundamental difference between Members of Parliament and all other staff members is that we are elected by the people. We are responsible to the people, and the people must have the final say on whether we come here in the first place, when we leave and how we leave.'

The principle of democratic accountability is fundamental to our system of representative democracy. But the argument frequently advanced by politicians – that the ballot box is the only mechanism by which elected office-holders should be held to account – is often disingenuous. It is well established that, under the UK's first-past-the-post parliamentary system, the vast majority of electors vote on the basis of party rather than casting their ballot for a particular individual.[8] This means that even a proven instance of personal misbehaviour is highly unlikely to sway the decision of most voters when they next complete a ballot paper – which could be four or five years hence. Equally, an MP's day-to-day efforts on behalf of their constituents – dealing with potholes or defending a local hospital – might lead voters to disregard reports of bad behaviour – a 'get out' clause unavailable to non-MPs who behave inappropriately. The fact that MPs subject themselves to democratic accountability at the ballot box should not justify them being exempt from the rules, processes and sanctions that are in place to enforce the standards we expect of people who choose to be in public life. But, as I discuss later in this chapter, MPs have sometimes stretched the principle of democratic accountability beyond its true purpose – using it to justify exempting themselves from their proper financial and employment responsibilities, which are distinct from their democratic role.

As well as being the elected representatives of the people, MPs are obviously exceptional because of the powers they collectively hold – to control taxes and government spending and – together with members of the House of Lords – to pass laws. Alongside the parliaments of Wales and Scotland, and the Northern Ireland Assembly, to which various legislative and tax-setting powers have been devolved – the Commons and the Lords are the only national institutions with these significant powers. The SNP MP Pete Wishart told me that for many MPs, Brexit had heightened the psychological significance of their legislative powers. The emphasis on the return from Brussels of law-making powers had 'emboldened a better conceit of ourselves and further strengthened our view that we are special'.

Bound up with these powers, and essential to the two houses of parliaments' ability to use them, are the 'privileges' asserted by parliament and accepted over time by the Crown and the courts. The word 'privileges' is a confusing term because it implies special treatment for MPs; it is perhaps better understood as 'protections' for the work of parliament. Erskine May defines parliamentary privilege in a way which explicitly sets MPs apart from the rest of the population – as 'the sum of certain rights enjoyed by each House collectively ... and by Members of each House individually, without which they could not discharge their functions, *and which exceed those possessed by other bodies or individuals*'[9] (emphasis added).

The purpose of the privileges afforded to MPs individually is to ensure that they can do their jobs so that collectively the House of Commons can fulfil its functions. Probably the most significant individual privilege is that of freedom of speech in debate. This is the ancient principle that the government should not take action against an MP for what he or she says in the course of parliamentary proceedings.[10] Today, the practical effect of this privilege is that MPs cannot be prosecuted for what they say in the Commons. This is important because it means that they can speak on behalf of their constituents without fear of being charged with libel, slander or any criminal offence, as can witnesses giving evidence to select committees. The privilege of freedom of speech places an important responsibility upon parliamentarians not to use it inappropriately – which occasionally leads to controversy, as when Boris Johnson, speaking under protection of privilege, accused Keir Starmer, when Director of Public Prosecutions, of failing to prosecute Jimmy Savile for child sex abuse. The privilege also puts MPs and peers under an obligation not to mislead the House – and to correct the record if they do so inadvertently.

There are also privileges which belong to the Commons and the Lords collectively. These are intended to protect members and reinforce the authority of each House. In theory, the Commons and Lords have the power to punish individuals who commit an offence against their House ('a contempt'). The reality of this power – and the limits of privilege – are less clear-cut. The absence of consequences for Dominic Cummings for refusing – despite an official summons – to give evidence to the Committee on Digital, Culture, Media and Sport regarding his role during the EU referendum as Director of 'Vote Leave', highlighted the Wizard-of-Oz nature of the House of Commons' power to enforce its will. Even though Cummings was found 'in contempt' of the House and formally admonished, he was subsequently given free access to the estate as a Special Adviser to Boris Johnson. And when he offered later to give evidence on the government's handling of Covid-19 he was welcomed back to do so.

A further privilege – the right of the Commons to 'exclusive cognisance' over its own precincts and proceedings[11] – was the power that Rees-Mogg described in his speech opening the debate on the Independent Expert Panel as 'Our ancient right that we should look after our own affairs'. Parliamentarians have this right because, under the UK's constitution, parliament is seen as having 'supremacy' over the other key institutions of the state – the executive cannot tell parliament what to do[12] and nor can the courts interfere in what goes on in parliament. Over time an understanding (or 'comity') has developed between judges and parliamentarians as to their respective areas of jurisdiction, so only parliamentarians can make decisions about how parliament should regulate its own proceedings. That said, it is also quite clear that privilege does not override the criminal law.[13]

... but not that special

In many ways then, MPs are in a unique position, and our constitution rightly grants them particular protections to ensure they can fulfil their democratic role. But it is also right that there should be limits to their exceptional status. It is important – not least to promote adherence to the rule of law by members of the public – that most Acts of Parliament should apply to MPs in exactly the same way as they do to their constituents – that MPs are not seen to be 'above' the laws that they pass for others. Unfortunately, the behaviour of parliamentarians too frequently implies a belief in the 'specialness' of MPs which goes beyond that which is warranted by the rules and conventions of the constitution.

Sometimes this is manifest in small ways: how MPs treat their staff or behave in front of witnesses to select committees – the 'don't you know who I am?' syndrome. In other instances, the behaviour is more public and egregious, such as when the SNP MP Margaret Ferrier decided to take a four-hour train journey back to her constituency in Rutherglen after having received a positive diagnosis of Covid-19. Cumulatively, such behaviour has a damaging effect on the credibility of MPs individually and the House of Commons collectively – as the *Daily Mail* headline raged following the Ferrier case: 'One rule for them! With quarter of UK plunged into local lockdown, MP ignores test and brings Covid to Commons'.[14] In 2021, similar complaints of exceptionalism were prompted by allegations about former Prime Minister David Cameron's lobbying on behalf of the failed finance firm Greensill Capital – and by the Johnson government's efforts to ensure that Owen Paterson MP would not face the consequences of his breaches of Commons rules on paid lobbying.[15]

Parliament has chosen to restrict some of its own privileges, sometimes through convention and sometimes through law. For example, both Houses have a longstanding convention known as the *sub judice* rule which prevents MPs and peers from referring to matters that are currently being decided in the courts.[16] Although, in principle, the privilege of freedom of speech means there is nothing to stop MPs referring to live legal cases without repercussions, parliamentarians have decided that they should exercise a self-denying ordinance to avoid prejudicing cases and trampling on the jurisdiction of the courts.

Over time, the two Houses have also accepted some limits on their right to self-regulation, particularly in relation to administrative matters. This has happened as changing societal norms have begun to diverge from those sustained by parliament's historical practices. As parliament has legislated to provide rights to individuals and compel organisations to meet certain administrative requirements – for example of transparency, financial probity and human resource management – the exceptions maintained for legislators have become increasingly visible and anomalous. And attempts to justify these exceptions on the grounds of parliament's privileges have become increasingly questionable.

Some anomalies have been ironed out. But often not because parliamentarians have recognised the importance of adhering to the standards that they have set for others. Instead, the two Houses have had to be forced to accept limitations on their own self-governance as the result of bad behaviour, scandals and resulting public opprobrium. Unfortunately, rather than acting as an exemplar, the impression is often that parliament has to be dragged into the modern era.

Some examples will illustrate the point. In 1994, the 'Cash for Questions' scandal, in which a series of MPs were accused of having accepted payments for the tabling of parliamentary questions, was the tipping point which prompted the then-Prime-Minister, John Major, to establish the Committee on Standards in Public Life in a last-ditch effort to address mounting accusations of 'sleaze' against his government. What became known as the 'Nolan committee' (after its chair) made a series of influential recommendations, including the creation of a post of Parliamentary Commissioner for Standards to oversee members' interests, and investigate complaints of breaches of the MPs' Code of Conduct. In this way, MPs flouting the rules (that they had set for themselves) triggered a scandal which compelled the

House of Commons to limit its own self-governance. Although the Commons held on to the right of MPs to take final decisions on the outcome of the Parliamentary Commissioner's investigations, it conceded the need to delegate the power for an unelected official to investigate breaches of the House's rules.[17]

A decade later, it was the attempt by the Conservative MP David Maclean (with the tacit support of the government) to pass a private Members' bill exempting MPs' and peers' correspondence from the provisions of the Freedom of Information (FOI) Act which triggered the MPs' expenses scandal. The Act – passed in 2000 – provides public access to information held by public authorities. But after some embarrassing disclosures of members' travel expenses early in 2007, many MPs – including ministers – concluded it was a bad Act and backed Maclean's bill – which would have prevented future releases relating to MPs and peers.

As the Liberal Democrat MP Norman Baker observed despairingly during the passage of the bill, 'This makes us look smug, self-serving and out of touch and eager to cloak ourselves in secrecy. It is effrontery for the House of Commons to make the deeply hypocritical move of exempting itself from a law that applies to every other public body in the country.'[18] Following a public outcry, no member of the House of Lords saw fit to sponsor the Maclean bill – a prerequisite for it to progress through the Upper House – and its progress was halted.

But the damage to the reputation of parliament had already been done. And the attempt to cover up the details of the expenses MPs were claiming from the public purse only fuelled interest in the story. As the academic Ben Worthy has shown, the eventual explosive leak of thousands of claims in 2009 was precipitated by a further series of FOI requests which led to the collation of all MPs' expense claims into a single record.[19] Meanwhile a drawn-out process of appeal and counter-appeal to the Information Tribunal, driven by MPs' resistance to disclosure and the impression created of a secretive internal Commons culture, kept the issue in the public eye, incentivising the eventual leaking of at least one million claims and their sensational-ised publication by the *Daily Telegraph* over a period of weeks.

While most of the rule infringements revealed by the leak were minor, some led to criminal prosecutions – further damaging the reputation of House of Commons. What was worse, some of the parliamentarians who were taken to court tried to argue that they should be immune from prosecution for crimes which would have seen their constituents convicted under the Theft Act 1968.

Before their trials on charges of false accounting, three MPs – Elliot Morley, David Chaytor and Jim Devine – and one member of the Lords – Lord Hanningfield – claimed that they could not be prosecuted because this would infringe their privileges as parliamentar-ians – breaching the principles that parliamentary proceedings should not be questioned in a court and that parliament should have exclusive cognisance over its own affairs. Their argument was that the claiming of parliamentary expenses was a proceeding of parliament, just like speaking in a debate or asking a minister a question. The public was astonished – the papers were full of outraged comparisons between 'privileged' MPs (the misunderstood term adding to the general dismay) and ordinary employees.

In the case of R v Chaytor, the Supreme Court disagreed with the parliamentarians' argument that false accounting laws should not apply to them, and dismissed their appeals. The judgments drew a distinction between decisions about matters relating to parliamentary administration taken by parliamentary committees (which were protected by privilege) and the administrative implementation of those decisions (which were not). Six MPs were eventually convicted of offences connected with their expense claims. Public outrage at MPs' misuse of their expenses was so great that it led to the resignation of the Commons Speaker, Michael Martin – who had himself been accused of misusing expenses. He was replaced by John Bercow (despite the fact he himself had been found to have 'flipped' his main and constituency homes, maximising his expense entitlement[20]).

The government felt compelled to draw a line under the damaging furore by conceding a further restriction on the Commons' right to regulate itself. Then Justice Secretary Jack Straw MP introduced the Parliamentary Standards Bill which handed over the power to set and administer the pay and allowances of MPs to a new independent body – the Independent Parliamentary Standards Authority (IPSA). Passed swiftly ahead of the 2010 election, the new Act gave IPSA the power to investigate possible breaches of the rules (and impose sanctions) and created a new criminal offence of providing false or misleading information for allowances claims, punishable by a fine and/or up to twelve months' imprisonment.

The Recall of MPs Act 2015 now means that any custodial sentence imposed on an MP for submitting a false claim gives his or her constituents the right to sign a petition to trigger a by-election, as happened to the Conservative MP for Brecon and Radnorshire, Christopher Davies, in 2019. Following his conviction for a misleading expense claim, Davies lost his seat in a by-election triggered by a petition signed by 18.9 per cent of his constituents, although he was subsequently reselected to fight the 2019 election (unsuccessfully). By contrast, DUP MP Ian Paisley Jr escaped recall after breaking Commons rules on paid advocacy because only 9.4 per cent of registered voters in his North Antrim constituency chose to sign his recall petition.

Self-regulation breeds misbehaviour

The privilege of parliamentary self-regulation is an essential part of our constitution. As discussed, it prevents the courts or the government interfering in decisions that are rightly for the legislature. But the existence of the privilege of exclusive cognisance can also have damaging effects on parliament. This is for two reasons.

First, the wish of parliamentarians to protect their right to manage their own affairs, has too often led to the preservation of inadequate administrative processes which have facilitated bad behaviour. Prior to the cash for questions scandal, most MPs believed they should be responsible for their own standards processes. But bad behaviour was facilitated by the absence of effective, independent processes for investigating and sanctioning breaches of the MPs' code of conduct; the long existence of a register of MPs' interests having done nothing to prevent the scandal. The principle of self-regulation had provided a ready excuse for maintaining the status quo.

Similarly, before the Freedom of Information Act came into force in 2005, there was an unexamined assumption that the House of Commons' important right to protect its private proceedings – such as the deliberations of MPs in a committee meeting – extended to the administration of MPs' expenses. As expense claims and processes for dealing with them were not exposed to the glare of public scrutiny, the incentive to ensure that processes were robust and rules were strictly enforced was reduced. Some of the most egregious claims submitted – for moat cleaning and duck houses – were actually refused by the Commons administration (a detail missed in much of the feverish media coverage). But the fact that MPs thought they might conceivably be permissible tells you a lot about their expectations of a system which had evolved to deliver on the wishes of MPs rather than to protect the taxpayer.

Prior to recent reforms, the same detrimental impact of self-regulation was evident in relation to bullying and harassment in the House of Commons. Historically, allegations against MPs were dealt with via informal, internal processes. Any sanctions – which were rare – were dealt with privately by the party whips who had little incentive to discipline their members, much less to do so in public. Attempts in the 2010s to introduce formal processes – including a so-called 'Respect' policy – disintegrated on first contact with MPs' exceptionalism, facilitated by the subservience of the House's administration. Until the #MeToo wave broke on Westminster in the autumn of 2017, politicians had no incentive to change processes which made it very unlikely they, or their party, would suffer the consequences of inappropriate behaviour. And the long-standing principle of parliamentary self-regulation made it very easy to justify their inertia.

The second reason that an emphasis on parliamentary self-governance has proven problematic is because of the psychological effect it has on some parliamentarians. In any group of 650 people there will always be a spectrum of ethical behaviour, although it is reasonable to suspect that MPs as a group are more comfortable with risk-taking than the population at large. As the former Conservative MP Matthew Parris has written – individuals drawn to elected office 'On the whole, by and large, and with any number of exceptions ... are driven men and women: dreamers, attention-seekers and risk-takers with a dollop of narcissism in their natures.'[21] At the same time, a senior backbencher remarked to me, 'Lots of MPs are frustrated; they come from being a very big fish in their constituency and discover they are a very small fish in a big pond in Westminster.'

The combination of these psychological effects can be problematic: some MPs feel their status gives them the right to be demanding or throw their weight around. Others may be tempted to actually break the rules. In each of the examples above, the knowledge that there was no external authority that might investigate or sanction them presumably emboldened MPs who were predisposed to drift to the wrong side of the ethical line to do so: accepting donations in return for asking questions, submitting questionable expense claims, or behaving inappropriately towards their staff.

The vast majority of MPs are neither 'angels' nor 'demons', but the 'exceptional' status of the House can have a damaging effect even for them – removing the reference point of external norms by which they might judge the acceptability of their behaviour. In each of these cases, the influence of the principle of exclusive cognisance partly explains the inappropriate actions of some MPs. It is sadly ironic that a principle which is so essential to the functioning of parliament should also have such a detrimental impact on the reputation of the individual MPs involved and the institution itself.

The palace is an exception

Another factor which promotes a sometimes inappropriate sense among MPs of their 'special' status, and which damages the reputation of the House of Commons, is the peculiar status of the building in which parliament meets – the Palace of Westminster.

Although the English parliament has sat in the Palace of Westminster since 1295 and Edward VI handed over St Stephen's chapel for the use of the Commons as far back as 1547, the current neo-gothic building is relatively modern – having been opened by Queen Victoria in 1852. But curiously, despite having been rebuilt specifically for the use of parliament following a catastrophic fire in 1834, the building remains a royal palace. This is even though it has not been a royal residence since 1529 when ... a catastrophic fire forced Henry VIII to move up the road to the Palace of Whitehall (are you spotting a pattern?).

In the Westminster system, parliament is understood to be composed of three parts – the Crown, the House of Lords and the House of Commons. Nonetheless, it is unusual for a parliament to sit in a building so closely connected with the monarchy – most parliaments around the world meet in their own dedicated premises. The fact that the Houses of parliament meet in the Palace of Westminster is a product of history, but arguably not integral to the operation of parliament. This is demonstrated by proposals for both Houses to move out of the palace to allow for the restoration of the building – which I discuss in Chapter 5. All that is needed for the Commons to meet wherever it chooses – somewhat bizarrely – is the presence of the mace – a silver-gilt ornamental club of about one-and-a-half metres in length, dating from the reign of Charles II – which is the symbol of royal authority.

Nonetheless, the royal status of the building in which the House of Commons meets is, for many MPs, closely bound up with the identity of the institution itself. This is clear from the frequency with which the 'royal palace' is referred to in debate as an integral aspect of parliament. During a debate on the restoration of the palace in July 2020, for example, Jacob Rees-Mogg argued that members must meet 'our collective responsibility of protecting this building, the throne, the palace of our democracy'.[22]

As well as stimulating feelings of awe and historic nostalgia among its members and the wider public, the fact that parliament sits in a royal palace has legal consequences. One example is that bars and restaurants on the parliamentary estate are exempt from levying duty on alcoholic drinks. Another is that the health and safety laws which govern other workplaces – including the Health and Safety at Work Act 1974 – do not apply to the Palace of Westminster (or other royal residences) and are respected by choice rather than compulsion.[23] Fire extinguishers on the estate are silver – not red – and fire-exit signs may use a different font to those in any other public building, but in most other ways, such legislation is scrupulously applied.

Some MPs are acutely aware that the palace is exempt from certain laws – which enhances their sense of their own exceptional status. During the Covid-19 pandemic, this fact was raised by MPs debating how to achieve social distancing in the chamber. Giving evidence to the Commons Procedure Committee, the Conservative MP Steve Brine stated, 'This is a royal palace for a start, so we are not bound by [Public Health England's] rules; we take their advice.' He was challenged by the Labour

MP Angela Eagle. '[B]ut surely we should be setting an example to everyone else,' she argued. 'If the people who make the laws and people who hold the government to account are obviously [not following the rules] ... we cannot expect the rest of the country to take the advice, can we?'[24]

It was a good question. Particularly during the early months of the pandemic, MPs were divided over the question of whether they should be sitting in Westminster at all and the message that their presence or absence would send to the public. After a brief period of hybrid in-person/virtual sittings and remote voting in May 2020, the government decided that MPs needed to set an example that normal life was resuming by returning to the House of Commons and voting in person. But many MPs felt that travelling backwards and forwards to their constituencies and queuing up around the parliamentary estate to vote in person set a perverse example to the public who – at the time – were being asked by ministers to 'work from home if you can' and maintain the 'two-metre rule'. The sight of MPs queueing up around the parliamentary estate in order to vote – often failing to observe social distancing – sent a contradictory message to their constituents and was widely ridiculed in the UK and international press.[25] Adding to the confusion about why parliament had returned, the British public could not see the problem with remote voting – a YouGov poll found that just 12 per cent of people thought that MPs should be required to be physically present in the House of Commons to vote while the Covid-19 pandemic was ongoing, and

35 per cent would have been happy for members to keep voting remotely once the pandemic was over.[26] MPs are far more persuaded of the importance of conducting their business in the Palace of Westminster than many of their constituents.

What should change?

In June 2020, a senior official giving evidence to MPs on the Procedure Committee reminded them that, 'As an organisation, the House has said that, whether or not it is formally bound by various forms of statute law – health and safety being one of those forms of statute law – it is none the less committed to abiding by it.' Just because it was possible for MPs to ignore the advice of Public Health England on social distancing it did not mean that they should, he implied, not least because 'the House would not wish to depart from what is perceived to be the guidance that the rest of the country is being advised to follow'.[27] The risk he warned against – of allowing a double standard to develop between MPs and the public – is a constant threat to the reputation of the House of Commons, and not just in relation to the Palace of Westminster.

The role of an MP is exceptional, and the powers, privileges and exemptions granted to elected Members exist for particular reasons – to protect their ability to fulfil their important role. But some MPs confuse their rights and privileges with a broader state of exception.

As well as tempting individual MPs to behave inappropriately, parliament's emphasis on its own uniqueness is a problem for MPs collectively. It inhibits them from modernising their administrative processes, from acknowledging the areas in which self-governance is no longer appropriate and from updating unnecessarily arcane rules (as I discussed in Chapter 3). At best this prolongs inefficient and outdated working practices; at worst it facilitates behaviour which can undermine the institution. The case of Owen Paterson MP, and the abortive attempt of the Johnson government to change the rules under which he had been found guilty of paid advocacy, have rightly prompted reflection about the House's standard processes and rules on MPs' outside interests. It is essential that MPs use this opportunity to think about improvements which would enhance public trust in the House of Commons, rather than relying on old assumptions about exceptions for elected members. They should look beyond parliament at the way in which other professions with a particular status regulate their activities – at doctors and barristers for example – to learn from the experience of others who are unique but – like MPs – cannot be exempt from ethical and administrative standards.

MPs need to be honest with themselves and the public about the actual purposes for which their powers, privileges and exemptions have been granted and recognise the proper boundaries that these place around their exceptional status. One way in which they might ground themselves in these realities would be to become less Westminster-centric – to more frequently and regularly spend time conducting parliamentary business outside the rarefied confines of the Palace of Westminster. This could be facilitated by the introduction of a monthly 'committee week' during which MPs on select committees could travel outside London to gather evidence for their inquiries without being concerned about missing crucial business in the chamber. Taking parliament to the people in this way would also have benefits for public perceptions of parliament – watching select committees at work is (normally) an edifying process and might go some way to dispelling cynicism about MPs' lack of interest in parts of the UK beyond south-east England.

The credibility of the House of Commons as an effective institution is undermined by the difficulty it seems to experience in identifying what it needs to change and achieving that change by itself. Where reforms have been pushed through, it is almost always because of a crisis or the intervention of external actors – investigative journalists, independent inquiries or other outside organisations. As I discussed in Chapter 3, the House of Commons needs to establish standing mechanisms for more regular and comprehensive review of its administrative and procedural processes, which cannot be immediately stymied by government's preference for the status quo. This is crucial to dispel the impression that MPs have to be dragged kicking and screaming into any instance of reform and that the House of Commons remains an exclusive club run primarily for the benefit of its members. In the next chapter I explore the consequences of this institutional inertia for the building in which parliament meets – the Palace of Westminster itself.

5

Decaying

Introduction

The Palace of Westminster is falling down. Literally. In the decade from 2009 to 2019 there were 14 recorded instances of masonry falling from the nineteenth-century buildings. In 2018, a chunk of a stone angel the size of a football fell 70 metres from the Victoria Tower into a garden below.[1] Luckily nobody was hurt. It is miraculous that nobody has yet been killed or seriously injured by falling stonework on the parliamentary estate, although in 2017 the window of a parked car was smashed by a tumbling piece of parapet.[2]

The history of attempts to restore the Palace of Westminster is a litany of dithering, buck-passing and delay which illustrates many of the themes already discussed in this book. The absence of a single point of parliamentary leadership means no one has been able to drive the work forward, while the complex governance of parliament as an institution has created numerous roadblocks and frequent reversals. Privileging their own short-term interests and preferences rather than seeing themselves as stewards of a national institution, successive generations of MPs have refused to acknowledge the gravity of the problems that need fixing. A constitutional set-up which privileges stability and an executive-dominated system have provided further brakes on progress and innovation.

In some ways it is unsurprising that parliamentarians have not grasped the nettle of restoring the palace. The project – if it ever takes place – will be difficult, time-consuming and expensive. A 'high-level estimate of the broad order of magnitude of the cost', calculated in 2014, posited a figure of £3.52 billion for work beginning in 2025. Although there has been no revised official estimate of the cost since 2014, by 2021, the likely figure had ballooned to £12 billion.[3] Every time the restoration is halted or put on the back burner, it simply gets more difficult, more time-consuming and more expensive, while the risk to the palace and those who work there grows.

The significance of the failure to restore the Palace of Westminster goes far beyond an overdue and expensive building project. There is an extensive literature on the way in which the physical design of a building influences what happens within it, and parliamentary buildings are no different. The American academic Charles Goodsell has argued that legislative buildings condition the thoughts and actions of people in three ways: 'they perpetuate the past, they manifest the present and they condition the future'.[4] Nowhere is this truer than in Westminster: the way in which politics is conducted today has been shaped by the architecture of the Palace of Westminster – with spaces that exclude 'outsiders' and maintain hierarchies among 'insiders'. As the academic Alex Meakin has argued, the design of the Palace of Westminster affects how parliamentarians and the public perceive their roles and the actions they take.[5] The disinclination of today's politicians to renovate the palace means that historical choices will continue to condition future behaviours and decisions in intended and unintended ways.

As the journalist Charlotte Higgins has observed, the Palace of Westminster is not inviting to visitors, being 'all too obviously a remnant of a pre-democratic age … built not to welcome its populace in, but to impress them with its fortress-like grandeur'.[6] By contrast, the Scottish parliament and Senedd in Wales – built in the last two decades – were consciously designed to shape the relationship between politicians and the public in quite different ways. The designer of the Senedd building in Cardiff, Lord Rodgers of Riverside, has described how the chamber was deliberately sunk beneath the public space, establishing a hierarchy between members and staff which 'deliberately reflects how politics should operate. … Transparency, for passers-by and visitors, and for the people watching the democratic debates below, is the driving force.'[7] The architecture of the Palace of Westminster reflects a time when politics was seen quite differently.

Very recently, the physical changes forced on Westminster by the Covid-19 pandemic – including the alterations made to the chamber and committee rooms to allow for remote participation and social distancing – illustrated some of the ways in which Westminster's physical environment shapes its politics. The decision to limit the number of MPs who could be present in the chamber to just 50, due to social distancing, completely changed the dynamics of set-piece proceedings such as Prime Minister's Questions – making them much quieter, more sober events than when 400-plus members used to cram into the space. The prohibition in both Houses on the use of the voting lobbies, due to inadequate ventilation, changed the extent and nature of participation in votes – with far more peers casting their votes in the online divisions held in the Lords and some MPs behaving less predictably than their whips would have liked in the Commons. And the move of select committees into virtual committee rooms led to changes in their selection of witnesses – enabling individuals more distant from Westminster to give evidence. The pandemic has unexpectedly provided us with evidence of the ways in which parliament's physical surroundings affect the way politics is 'done' in Westminster.

In this chapter I discuss the problems that have dogged the project to restore the Palace of Westminster and the consequences – actual and potential – of parliamentarians' refusal to allow it to proceed. The problems, I argue, are symptomatic of wider issues which are undermining public trust in the House of Commons which need to be addressed in order to reverse the spiral of decline in public confidence in Parliament. While the failure to proceed with the project has perpetuated a practical risk – eventually the delay will inevitably prove fatal to one or more unlucky individuals or lead to the accidental destruction of the palace – MPs' failure to make the House of Commons more diverse, comprehensible and modern has created a more existential risk – to parliament's credibility and relevance as an institution. As others, including the former Commons Speaker, John Bercow, have argued, rather than shying away from the decision, MPs should seize the restoration as an opportunity for an open conversation with the public about what Parliament is for and how it should operate in the twenty-first century.[8] This conversation could be the starting point for the reversal of the spiral of declining confidence in which Parliament finds itself.

The crumbling palace

If you work on, or visit, the parliamentary estate, a lump of stone angel falling on your head is not the only risk that you have to contend with. Ironically, given that the palace was built after the previous building was almost completely destroyed by a blaze in 1834,[9] and the earlier history of the site was marked by numerous fires, a Notre-Dame-style conflagration remains an ever-present danger.

Between 2017 and 2019, despite the teams of fire wardens who patrol the parliamentary estate twenty-four hours a day, nineteen fires were found (and extinguished!) in the Commons[10] and three in the Lords.[11] In one case a fire was nearly caused by a different maintenance problem – water leaking through the ceiling of the Peers'

Writing Room dripped onto an electrical socket in the floor, causing an arc of sparks and fumes.

Some aspects of the palace's deterioration have, so far, been more a matter of inconvenience than mortal hazard. Into this category we could certainly put the audacious mice who used to join me in the office when I was working late and the rampant clothes moths who not only nibbled all the historic furnishings at work but also hitched a lift home and bred enthusiastically among my favourite woollies. The arrival of a cat on the estate – belonging to Sir Lindsay Hoyle, the current Speaker – may make a small dent on the rodent problem, but the lepidopteral invasion has proven hard to restrain in a palace full of delicious carpets and tasty Pugin-patterned curtains.

But many other aspects of decay on the parliamentary estate are potentially much more serious. Unsurprisingly given the Victorian pipework that survives throughout the palace, water leakage is commonplace. Incidents range from the innocuous, to the expensive (leaking rainwater has damaged the ceiling above central lobby), to the deeply unpleasant (sewage dripping through the ceiling into MPs' offices). These problems are not surprising when you consider the age of the infrastructure: in the basement of the palace lurks a sewage ejector, installed in 1888, which is still operating today.

In 2019 a flood of water into the Commons chamber, caused by a water leak in the Press Gallery two floors above, provided a foretaste of the possible disruption which could be caused by a more significant incident. As water poured into the Chamber, Labour MP Justin

Madders quipped: 'I hope I can complete my speech before rain stops play. I think there's probably some kind of symbol there about how broken Parliament is.' The sitting had to be suspended two hours early and the Press Gallery canteen was forced to close.[12]

The palace is also riddled with asbestos. Mostly this is not an active problem because it is trapped behind panels or contained in the numerous 'risers' (vertical shafts which carry pipes, cables and wires between the floors of the building). But it makes any restoration efforts much harder because workers have to take precautions against inhaling the damaging fibres. The presence of asbestos also increases the risk associated with any major fire or an explosion which might result from the rupture of an ancient steam pipe or boiler.

The possibility of such an explosion is one of the major risks which keeps officials responsible for maintaining the palace awake at night. But dealing with the antiquated plumbing which runs through the basement is far from straightforward. The original Victorian boilers which sit under the Commons and the Lords are not only operating decades beyond their expected life, they are also listed. Their listing means that even if they are decommissioned, they cannot be removed from their original location. So new boilers will have to be squeezed in beside them or the whole system will have to be relocated.

The task of maintaining the deteriorating palace was compared by a parliamentary committee in 2016 to 'trying to fill a bathtub with a thimble while the water is draining out of the plughole at the other end'.[13] The running repairs required are numerous and complex – some, like the restoration of the rare Victorian encaustic tiles which line the floor of Central Lobby, require highly specialised craftspeople, who are in short supply.[14] The annual cost of repair and renovation of the palace has been growing, from around £30 million in 2007 to closer to £50 million in 2015.[15] By three years later, in 2018/19, the figure had almost tripled to £127 million a year. In March 2021, a strategic review of the work required to renovate the palace found that 'The 150-year-old building is falling apart faster than it can be fixed.'[16] Over 40,000 maintenance problems were reported between 2017 and 2020.[17]

A project to restore a huge, world-famous and unique heritage building, located in the middle of London, to a challenging timescale (in order to minimise the disruption to parliamentary business) would be an extraordinarily difficult task at the best of times. The fact that the Palace of Westminster is the active home of the UK's parliament makes it many times harder.

The upkeep of the palace is constrained by the presence of its large and highly mobile working population. Many kinds of works are impossible while the two chambers are sitting. Repairs have to be done in fits and starts, squeezed into weekends and recesses when parliamentarians are at home or in their constituencies. The longest stretch of time available to maintenance teams each year is the summer recess. Visit parliament during August and the place is a very different hive of activity from during 'term time'. To get from one end of the palace to the other you must pick your way through courtyards full of scaffolding, down corridors of exposed floorboards with carpets rolled back to the walls and past holes with clusters of pipework and bundles of electrical wiring exposed. Contracts for work in the chamber have to include a clause that provides for the work to be abandoned and the chamber restored to its normal operating appearance within 24 hours in case there is a sudden recall of parliament. These constraints make any large-scale restoration work simply impossible while parliament is sitting at Westminster.

'Restoration and renewal'

To those familiar with the decrepit state of the palace and the constraints on conducting running repairs it has long been obvious that the situation is unsustainable. Discussions about what is today – optimistically – known as the 'restoration and renewal' (R&R) of the palace have been going on for at least thirty years. In 1990, an internal report argued it was 'essential' that 'a substantial amount of work' be done 'to bring the buildings and facilities up to reasonable standards'[18] and a survey of the palace basement found a significant amount of the mechanical and electrical infrastructure would need replacing in the next 10 to 15 years. Over the following three decades, repeated surveys and studies identified the inadequacy of annual maintenance efforts, recommended extensive works and highlighted substantial risks to the ongoing business of parliament if they were not undertaken. A series of inquiries and reviews came to the same conclusion – that the quickest and cheapest way to tackle the scale of work needed was for the building to be vacated – or 'decanted', in parliamentary parlance – for a period of years.

But despite these consistent recommendations, politicians were unable to agree on how to proceed. Successive generations of parliamentarians expertly chucked this hot potato onto the next – avoiding having to deal with either the inconvenience of moving out, or the cost, complexity and disruption of a restoration project. The academics Matthew Flinders, Leanne-Marie Cotter, Alix Kelso and Alex Meakin have argued that this prevarication has not just been a matter of lack of political will, but an example of a wider phenomenon in which political elites 'will generally reject or dilute reform agendas that threaten their privileged position within a constitutional configuration'.[10] They suggest that R&R represents a challenge to the way in which politics is done at 'Westminster' which threatens, and has therefore been resisted by, the two main political parties, who effectively hold vetoes over the work proceeding. The reason that the restoration project is seen as a threat is because it could alter the structures, procedures, design and culture of Parliament; elements which currently embed the UK's two-party system and an implicit hierarchy in which elected members rank above all other users of the palace.

Two steps forward, one step back

In the absence of political consensus on any form of decant to allow for significant R&R works, the patch and mend approach continued well into the twenty-first century. In May 2016, the Joint Committee on the Palace of Westminster – a special cross-party Commons and Lords committee set up to agree a way forward – finalised the latest in a long series of reports on the Palace. But the joint committee decided not to publish its final report in the furore ahead of the imminent EU referendum – fearing it would be too easy to ignore. Publication was then delayed again following David Cameron's resignation in the wake of the Brexit vote and the Conservative leadership contest which it triggered. This meant that the joint Committee's report – which argued for a full decant – allowing an army of electricians, plumbers, builders, stonemasons and engineers completely free rein to undertake their work – did not appear until September 2016. The committee's conclusion – that there was 'a clear and pressing need to tackle the work required to the Palace of Westminster and to do so in a comprehensive and strategic manner to prevent catastrophic failure in the next decade' – was in line with many previous studies, as was its finding that a full decant would be the cheapest and the most time efficient way to renovate the palace.

All that was needed at this point was for the government to provide an opportunity for the two Houses to debate the report and take a decision on its recommendations. This was originally expected to happen before Christmas 2016, but for eight months – until April 2017 – the government refused to commit to a date for the debate. Then the date it did propose fell victim to the dissolution of parliament ahead of the

2017 election. That October, Andrea Leadsom – the government minister responsible – committed to a debate before Christmas, which finally took place ... in January 2018.

Even in January 2018, 20 months after the joint committee had completed its report, the government attempted to prevent parliament taking a final decision on the project. Leadsom tabled two motions for the Commons to decide upon, both of which called for further reviews. She said that the motions could not be altered, but MPs ignored her and put forward amendments requiring MPs to either support or oppose decant.

The chair of the Public Accounts Committee, Labour MP Meg Hillier – someone with plenty of experience of dissecting tricky, major public-sector projects – proposed an amendment which signed the Commons up to the whole programme of restoration and renewal and a 'full and timely decant', as recommended by the joint committee. Unexpectedly, on 31 January, the Commons voted by 236 votes to 220 to accept the amendment and on 6 February the Lords followed suit.

By late 2019 it looked like real progress had finally been made. Against the odds, in the middle of parliament's Brexit agonies, the Parliamentary Buildings (Restoration and Renewal) Act 2019 was passed. The government made time for the Bill to pass through parliament and it was backed by a cross-party coalition of parliamentarians (before receiving Royal Assent twice – for good measure – due to Johnson's failed prorogation).

Becoming law nearly two years after parliament's decision to go ahead with the R&R project, the Act adopted the governance structures used to deliver major projects such as the 2012 Olympic Games. It established an independent 'Sponsor Body' made up of parliamentarians and external members to act as a 'client' on behalf of parliament, setting the scope, timeline and budget for the work, and an expert 'Delivery Authority' to take responsibility for delivering the R&R works.

However, following the 2019 election, a number of politicians began to cast doubt on whether the decision of the previous parliament to proceed with R&R should be allowed to stand. The new Speaker Sir Lindsay Hoyle suggested that MPs elected at the 2019 general election should have the opportunity to revisit the decision. Senior figures in the Conservative party – including the Leader of the House Jacob Rees-Mogg and chief whip Mark Spencer – made statements favouring backtracking on parliament's previous decisions – in particular on the idea of a full decant. As academic Alexandra Meakin has noted, only two of the 24 members of Boris Johnson's 2020 cabinet had voted in favour of the Hillier amendment in 2018, so ministerial support for a decant was weak.[20] By 2021, the political momentum appeared to have swung back behind either the idea of sticking with running repairs or going for a partial decant with a 'retained presence' – MPs continuing to use the chamber while works were under way.

A partial decant is not a simple solution. It would be orders of magnitude harder than a full decant, therefore slower and – according to the 2014 estimates – at least £1 billion more expensive. This is because nobody knows where most of the wires, pipes and cables that run through the palace go, or what they do. There is every chance that snipping a cable at one end of the palace will switch off the electricity or suspend broadcasting at the other. And that is quite apart from the noise and dust that will be generated, and the potential security risk of having numerous temporary contractors on site. Parliamentarians trying to carry on as normal while any significant programme of works was attempted around them would need to be prepared for serious disruption – in 2016, proceedings in the Lords chamber had to be suspended due to the noise of stonework cleaning outside. Worse still, an unexpected mishap could propel them into a sudden, unplanned evacuation.

In March 2021, the Sponsor Body published the results of a 'strategic review' of R&R examining whether changes in the context of the project warranted a change in approach. But this confirmed the conclusion of many previous reviews – that a full decant remained the best option. Continued partial occupation of the palace during the works would be 'technically possible' but import an 'extraordinary level of risk', extra time measured in 'decades' and far higher cost.[21] The Sponsor Body's report echoed the verdict of the 2016 Joint Committee report that a partial decant 'could turn out to combine the worst of all options'. Nonetheless, this apparently continues to be the current government's preferred way forward.

Why has the palace not been restored?

The simplest answer to the question of why R&R has not yet begun is, of course, the money. The price tag for the work is enormous and many MPs feel deeply uncomfortable about the prospect of justifying the cost of the project to their constituents. The idea of 'spending money on politicians' is politically tricky in any country at any time, but there are additional sensitivities in Westminster, intensified by the laser-like focus of the British media on the cost of politics.

Although the actual sums of money involved were small, memories of the MPs' expenses scandal remain fresh and, over a decade on, politicians remain conscious of the public perception that they are acting in their own self-interest. Ironically, the wish of MPs today to avoid being seen to spend money on themselves by getting on with R&R is motivated by a scandal created by precisely the same motive. MPs did not want to be seen to vote themselves higher salaries, so they relied instead on the short-term fix of allowances until abuse of the system led to its collapse in the conflagration of scandal.

Public concern about the cost of politics became particularly acute in the wake of the decade of austerity which followed the global financial crisis of 2007–08, and has now been exacerbated further by the hundreds of billions added to the public debt by the government response to the Covid-19 pandemic.[22] There are further sensitivities about making a significant infrastructure investment which is seen disproportionately to benefit the south-east of the UK, particularly as the Johnson government was elected on a manifesto promise to 'level-up' other regions of the country. This was presumably why Johnson floated the idea of moving the House of Lords to York – an idea subsequently examined and rejected by the Sponsor Body's 2021 Strategic Review.

But it is not just about the money. The indecision and deliberate delay surrounding the project reflect many of the other weaknesses of the House of Commons, including those discussed in previous chapters. One set of these relate to the characteristics of MPs themselves, another to the governance of the House of Commons and a third to the vested interests of the two main political parties. All have been intensified by one particular parliamentary convention – that no parliament can 'bind' its successors. This means that no decision on the R&R project can ever be considered final.

To begin with MPs themselves. It is a truism to say that politics is a short-term game, but it is highly relevant in this context. The public might hope that MPs would act as stewards of the House of Commons – making decisions about what is best for the institution in the long term, but few see that as their role. As the former Labour MP Tony Wright argued in 2004, 'there is no parliament, in that collective sense ... There are simply Members of Parliament who have preoccupations and inhabit a career structure in which attention to the sustained strengthening of the institution is not a central priority.'[23] Expending political capital on a project which will not come to fruition for decades is an unattractive prospect for an MP facing re-election within the next five years. This is particularly so when, for MPs today, the project is likely to have only downsides – the disruption of moving out of the palace, the inconvenience of operating from an alternative site and the almost inevitable political risk of escalating costs and delays associated with a project of this scale.

The exceptionalism of many MPs – discussed in Chapter 4 – intersects with the short-termism of politics. The fact that they meet in the Palace of Westminster is core to the parliamentary identity of many members, who fear a decline in prestige associated with meeting in an alternative location – even if this is nearby and for a limited period. A repeated concern expressed in debates on R&R is the prospect that once members move out of the Palace they will 'not be allowed back' due to project problems or overruns. It is undeniable that for some MPs this is a real prospect. The works will take at least a decade – probably longer – and so span more than one five-year Parliament. Having moved out, some MPs will lose their seats in intervening elections and never sit in the palace again. New MPs elected after the House has decanted might never sit in the palace at all, depending on the timing of elections and their own electoral prospects. These short-term realities clearly affect the views of individual MPs on R&R. Their undeclared preference is that a notional future cohort of MPs should take on the inconvenience and risk of the project. When it comes to the House of Commons, many MPs hold nostalgic, reactionary views underpinned by the benefits of the current set-up to themselves. While a long historical pedigree is often put forward as justification for retaining outdated structures and procedures, in practice the actual reason to oppose change is to maintain the structures, procedures, design and culture of parliament which benefit current MPs and their parties.

Some individual politicians have grasped the need for R&R and been willing to champion it despite the cost, inconvenience and difficulty of persuading their uninterested or vehemently opposed colleagues. Key amongst them have been certain Leaders of the House – the ministers responsible for relations between government and each House. Since the Leaders speak for the government within the parliamentary administration, their views have been crucial in determining whether the project has progressed during their tenure or gone into reverse. One example of a sceptic-turned proponent of the work is former Leader of the House, Andrea Leadsom MP, who told the House in July 2020, 'When I first looked at the issues of restoration and renewal, I started out with a healthy degree of scepticism … but I urge hon. Members who are lobbying for us to stay in the palace with no contingency arrangements and allow the vital work to go on all around us to accept that that is not realistic.'[24] But even though some Leaders have been supportive, rapid turnover in these rarely sought-after ministerial roles has hindered progress – there have been 18 Commons Leaders in the three decades since 1990 when serious efforts towards R&R began.

The second set of weaknesses which have beset the R&R project relate to the governance of parliament.

Because both the Commons and the Lords occupy the Palace of Westminster, both need to agree for the project to move forwards. But, as on many aspects of the running of parliament, decision-making has been hampered by the complex management structures of the two Houses and the absence of a single point of decision-making capable of driving forward a project of this scale.

For good constitutional reasons, the Commons and the Lords are funded and run independently – each having their own Management Board – but these bodies operate remarkably separately for two organisations sharing one premises. Each House provides similar services to its members but most of these are run separately, including the libraries, procedural services, human resources, catering and finance departments. When it comes to the maintenance of the parliamentary estate, the Commons and the Lords hold joint stewardship of the Palace of Westminster. The In-House Services department – which has responsibility for maintaining and restoring the estate – is part of the Commons administration but is jointly funded and accountable to both Management Boards.

If this was not complicated enough (and the entire management structure of the Commons has been reorganised on several occasions over the past three decades), the two management boards rarely get to make final decisions about the parliamentary estate. This is because they must ratify all significant decisions with their respective members. At a minimum, important decisions must be run past the Commission of each House – a kind of non-executive board chaired by the

Speaker (or Lord Speaker) and made up of members and non-executives (and – in the Commons only – two officials).[25] The two Commissions rarely meet jointly, and even when they do, the meetings only have formal status in the Commons because the rules of the Lords Commission do not allow for joint meetings. At a maximum, the most significant administrative decisions must be voted on by one or both Houses. Decisions about the restoration of the Palace of Westminster and consequences for the Commons and Lords fall very firmly into the latter category. So, however much parliamentary staff might wish to act as 'stewards' of parliament for the longer term, their freedom to do so is constrained by the decisions of today's politicians.

And there is greater complexity still, because the two Commissions do not take decisions alone. Each is advised by further committees of members. The Commons has one on 'Finance' and one on 'Administration'. The latter innocuous-sounding moniker disguises what can be an active and influential committee with a broad remit which ranges from the cost of a cup of tea in the Members' tearoom to major questions about the how the Commons should operate.[26] Most MPs and peers are not particularly interested in the administration of parliament. Those who choose to sit on the Finance and Administration Committees, and their equivalents in the Lords, are the exception.

Another significant interested party, when it comes to decisions about the parliamentary estate, is the monarch. This is because (as discussed in Chapter 4) the Palace of Westminster technically remains a royal palace. Used to a yearly trip to the House of Lords to 'open' parliament at the start of each annual parliamentary 'session', the sovereign has an important voice when it comes to decisions about restoring the palace. The main practical consequence of the palace's royal status is that the Lord Great Chamberlain – the sixth of the Great Officers of State – exercises control over certain parts of the building on behalf of the sovereign. This includes Westminster Hall – the vast hammer-beam-roofed hall which is one of the last surviving elements of the medieval palace. Still used for coronation banquets until the nineteenth century, Westminster Hall is now the setting for significant set-piece parliamentary events – including lyings-in-state and, in recent years, speeches by President Obama and Nelson Mandela.[27]

The decision in 2019 of the then Speaker, John Bercow, to veto the possibility of Donald Trump giving a speech in Westminster Hall during his state visit to the UK was controversial. Publicly this was because it was seen as a political intervention by a supposedly impartial Speaker. But privately Bercow's intervention was viewed as unfortunate because it pre-empted what would normally have been a joint decision about the use of Westminster Hall, made by the triumvirate of the Lord Great Chamberlain, Lord Speaker and Commons Speaker.

Beyond the monarch, there is a long list of external bodies who get a say in decisions on the palace. Westminster City Council takes a strong interest. As the palace is a Grade 1 listed building which, together with Westminster Abbey and St Margaret's Church, forms part of a UNESCO World Heritage Site, numerous conservation bodies, including English Heritage, Historic England and UNESCO, have a locus to get involved in even the smallest changes.

What all this means is that there has been no single point of parliamentary leadership which can simply push forward with a project of this kind. Instead, a sizeable minority of the people who work in the palace and some external organisations – all with differing priorities and interests – are veto players when it comes to decisions about whether and how to renovate the building. Over time, their many and varied motivations have dogged attempts to move ahead in a straight line with efforts to restore the palace.

Amongst these veto players, perhaps most significant in inhibiting R&R from progressing have been the two main political parties at Westminster who have vested interests in maintaining the status quo. Matthew Flinders and his colleagues have argued that the architecture and design of the Palace of Westminster were explicitly intended to embed a very specific type of politics – exclusionary, mystifying, hierarchical and adversarial – which today's main parties have an interest in maintaining.[28] The alternative – a more open, efficient, inclusive and outward-facing parliamentary building – would risk changing the culture, practices and symbolism of parliament in unpredictable ways which might not be to their benefit. Even the process of restoration, and the experience of parliament decanting into alternative facilities could establish different expectations among MPs and the public which might be contrary to their interests. During parliamentary consideration of R&R, representatives of vested party-political interests have deliberately closed down the options for the project, excluding the most radical possibilities, in order to avoid any challenge to their own privileged position.

What should change?

What the history of the R&R project demonstrates is how poor parliament's systems are for making long term decisions that stick about the institution itself and at balancing the needs of current members and political parties against those of others – including their potential successors and the wider public. As Matthew Flinders and his colleagues have observed, these shortcomings are compounded by the fact that 'there is no clear agreement amongst politicians of what is "wrong" with the Palace of Westminster (beyond obvious structural frailties) or what characteristics a parliament "that is fit for the twenty-first century" might look like'.[29] The public's views on this question have not been seen as significant.

It is not unexpected that a major project of this kind should need to balance competing interests. What has made decision-making on R&R particularly intractable has been that decisions have been taken by a constantly changing cast of MPs and in the context of the parliamentary convention that no parliament can bind its successors. This fundamental aspect of parliamentary sovereignty is usually discussed in relation to the laws that parliament makes, but it applies equally to internal decisions. In relation to R&R it means that no decision about the project – even the law passed to establish the Sponsor Board and Delivery Authority – can ever be regarded as final, because it could always be superseded by a subsequent decision. For a project with a timescale of decades which closely engages the interests of MPs, this convention has been crippling.

It is right, of course, that today's generation of MPs should have a say over the future of the building which they occupy. They have been elected by their constituents to make decisions about the running of the country and to sign off on government expenditure: the restoration of the Palace of Westminster requires both. However, the interests of today's members are by no means the only interests at play in decision making on R&R. And the refusal of many MPs to take responsibility for progressing the project reflects the tendency of some members and the main political parties to privilege their own interests and a romanticised view of the significance of the Palace of Westminster over the benefits of modernisation which might accrue to others. Interestingly, and contrary to what some might expect given the reputation of the House of Lords for conservatism, a majority of peers have consistently supported R&R (including a full decant).

As discussed in Chapter 2, current MPs are, by definition, a cohort who have chosen to stand for election to the House of Commons as it is currently configured – both in terms of its physical set-up and the way it conducts its proceedings. Logically, there must also exist a cohort who would have made brilliant MPs but who have looked at the role of a member of parliament and decided it was not for them. Among many possible reasons, this might be because of what they could see about parliament's physical environment. For example, academics Sarah Childs[30] and Karen Ross[31] have each explored how aspects of design, including even the artwork on the walls, have reinforced perceptions of parliament as a gendered space built by and for men.

It would not be surprising if an individual with a physical disability thought they would find the Palace of Westminster difficult to navigate. Although improvements have been made since the current Palace was completed in 1860, it remains very inaccessible – full of narrow corridors, flights of steps and ancient, diminutive lifts. Due to the layout of the Chamber, wheelchair users have to remain on the floor of the House next to the entrance. Even the act of voting normally requires MPs to move out of the chamber and back in again via the division lobbies, unless it has been agreed they can be 'nodded through' by their whips. Efforts have been made to accommodate current MPs who have disabilities – for example by finding them offices within the palace on the same floor as the Chamber – but these are in short supply.

The endless debates on R&R have focused almost entirely on the palace as the workplace of MPs and peers or as a heritage building to be protected, not as an institution belonging to the nation, to which citizens have a right of access. In this way, discussions about R&R echo the wider tendency of MPs to focus on their own preferences, rather than changing the House in ways that would make it more effective and welcoming to the public or help increase the diversity of future cohorts of MPs. Consideration of the needs of non-MPs has been largely absent from debates on R&R – MPs opposed to the idea that the restoration might change their established privileges and working practices and worried that improving accessibility might become an excuse for unnecessarily 'gold-plating' have argued that the current palace should simply be restored (not 'renewed'). It was only via Meg Hillier's amendment to the government's 2018 motion that the House instructed the Sponsor Body and Delivery Authority to 'include measures to ensure … the improvement of visitor access including the provision of new educational and other facilities for visitors and full access for people with disabilities'.[32]

This debate has still not been settled. The 2021 Strategic Review suggested that making the palace fully accessible would be a 'stretch' rather than 'essential' objective of the works.[33] In a debate in May 2021, Jacob Rees-Mogg signalled he would be happy with an only partially accessible building, saying, 'I hope that we can all agree on a cost-effective approach which provides disabled Members with accessible workplaces and visitors with access to the key democratic parts of this building', questioning 'whether we need disabled access "to all users to all areas of the building".'[34] It will be regrettable if MPs sign off on plans that will prevent people with certain disabilities from accessing parts of their own parliament.

The experience of Covid-19 is rightly prompting a rethink on R&R. For some MPs, the Covid-19 pandemic has brought home the health and safety downsides of working in nineteenth-century, neo-gothic palace, even for the fully able. Social distancing has proven tricky, especially in relation to voting – with the division lobbies in which MPs normally congregate (essentially wide corridors running on either side of the chamber) judged by Public Health England to be unsafe. After the government decided to discontinue a brief (and, technically, highly successful) experiment with remote voting, MPs had to queue around the estate in order to vote. Labour MP Hilary Benn told me that in-person voting had put the health of members and staff at risk: 'The House of Commons is now a really Covid-secure workplace, but the most unsafe thing we do is queue up to vote.' It is remarkable that MPs tolerated this inconvenience while a perfectly functioning, quick and reliable online alternative was available (and continued to be used by the House of Lords). It is also surprising that there was not more public concern about the democratic implications of the mass use of proxy voting – subsequently introduced to enable MPs who could not be physically present in Westminster to cast their votes.[35] By Easter 2021, 595 out of 650 MPs had signed up for a proxy vote – meaning that their votes were cast in person by just 18 nominated individuals – mostly party whips.[36] This undermined the significance of debate – the idea that MPs might change their minds about how to vote based on the views expressed by their colleagues – and made it harder for MPs to rebel against the party line.

The House's response to the pandemic set important precedents. It showed that it was possible for the Commons to carry out its work with most MPs absent from the chamber, for votes to be held remotely and for select committee to operate online. All of these innovations have implications for what decant accommodation would need to provide during R&R: MPs could potentially manage with a smaller chamber, without division lobbies and without a full complement of select committee rooms.

Members might not want to accept any of these compromises – moving proceedings online and holding votes remotely changed the dynamics of parliamentary business in ways which made some uncomfortable – but the experience of Covid-19 should challenge key assumptions about the R&R project. Major objections to decant made by proponents of the case to 'stay put and put up with the disruption' have been about the cost of reshaping Richmond House (the building adjoining the parliamentary estate on Whitehall to which the Commons would move), including demolishing much of the existing building to make way for a temporary chamber. The cost could be considerably reduced if MPs were prepared to move more of their proceedings online, and the need for dramatic changes to Richmond House could be reduced if remote voting meant division lobbies were not required.

It may be that these ways of reducing the cost of R&R prove unacceptable, or that new objections arise in their place. It would not be the first time. But while today's MPs may feel they have the right to tolerate the physical restrictions and historical oddities of the palace, it is wrong for them to allow their individual preferences to override the interests of the wider public. In doing so they are refusing to acknowledge the extent to which the architecture of the current palace affects the nature of the politics conducted within it and potentially prevents many people from visiting, working in or standing for election to the Commons, privileging their own short-term priorities over the institution's long-term interests.

What is certain is that the alternative to progressing with R&R will eventually be watching the palace crumble into the Thames, be destroyed by a huge fire or, over time, simply become an ever more anachronistic and inaccessible metaphor for the state of the UK's democracy. MPs should be using R&R as an opportunity for a wider public debate about what parliament is for and how it should operate in the twenty-first century – giving the public a say over the future of its own parliament. MPs might not be prepared to make the argument for spending billions on restoring the Palace of Westminster, but they should also consider how a Notre Dame-style fire rampaging through parliament will look to the world as a symbol of 'Global Britain'.

Conclusion: A parliament to be proud of

Introduction

It is not uncommon for MPs to express concern about the public's opinion of their profession and of the House of Commons. 'What must the watching public think?' is a common rhetorical device used in speeches – often to criticise a political opponent who has chosen an inconvenient subject for debate. But usually this is simply an oratorical flourish – not a serious diagnosis of a problem to be addressed. Few MPs take the time to actually identify the sources of the public's low opinion of the House of Commons, let alone take personal responsibility for addressing them.

Critically, few MPs think to locate the source of this low public esteem – at least part of it – in their own behaviour or the way they allow their institution to be run. It is much easier to ascribe the problem to the sweep of history and the peculiar nature of politics as a profession, than to attribute it to concrete issues which could be addressed in the here and now by changing their individual or collective behaviour or reforming the practices and procedures of the House.

But the public's poor opinion of the House of Commons is an issue that MPs should take seriously. Not only does it disparage them personally, but it also undermines their work – making it easier for the government to disregard their input and harder for them to achieve their goals. And when members of the public hold MPs in low regard, this makes them more likely to question MPs' effectiveness at holding the government to account and scrutinising its policies. In turn this undermines confidence in our system of government establishing a vicious cycle of decline in our key democratic institution.

This matters. Research shows that in countries with low trust in government, the public are less inclined to comply with rules and regulations, less keen to support government reforms and more risk-averse – all with negative consequences for society and the economy.[1] Low trust can also make the public less willing to engage with the processes of politics, leading to lower voter turnout at elections, which in turn chips away at the legitimacy of democratic institutions, contributing to the downward spiral of esteem and engagement.[2]

This problem is not new – the British public have long distrusted their politicians – but it is acute. In recent years trust in parliament has dropped as low as it has been in living memory. And while the problem is not unique to the UK – political institutions and especially elected bodies in most countries struggle to attract the confidence of the public – the existence of an international problem should not preclude a search for national answers. Not least because the Westminster parliament is one of the least trusted in Europe.

Some politicians are worried. The Conservative peer and academic Philip Norton has argued that, since Brexit, 'The change in terms of public perceptions of MPs is not simply one of degree, but of kind. Before, electors did not trust MPs. Now, they do not trust the House of Commons.'[3] But the fact that trust in politics is low internationally, and has been so for decades, has bred a dangerous complacency among too many of our political class. Alarming statistics – like the Hansard Society's 2019 finding that 42 per cent of the public thought that 'many of the country's problems could be dealt with more effectively if the government didn't have to worry so much about votes in parliament' – pass almost without comment in Westminster. The belief that ''twas ever thus' is a convenient excuse for inertia among MPs when it comes to addressing the problem.

'Familiarity breeds favourability, not contempt'

One reason that MPs may set aside concerns about trust in the House of Commons is because they themselves are convinced of the contribution that they – individually and collectively – are making. Recognising that the positive effects of the House of Commons on government are far more evident to those who work in and around Westminster than to the rest of the public, MPs are persuaded that better communicating the value of their work to their constituents is the best way to address their poor opinion of the House.

It is not unreasonable for MPs to want to develop public understanding of the work of the House of Commons. Nor is it wrong-headed. Roger Mortimore of IPSOS Mori observed in 2003, writing in the years following 'sleaze' allegations against John Major's government, that the strong correlation between familiarity with an institution and positive emotions towards it is as relevant to politicians and political institutions as it is to corporations and their brands. The marketing principle that 'familiarity breeds favourability, not contempt' is borne out by studies which show that if members of the public know the name of their local MP, they tend to perceive them more positively than they do MPs in general. In the five biannual surveys it conducted between 2004 and 2012, the Committee on Standards in Public Life found that respondents consistently had a more positive opinion of their local MP than of MPs as a group; in 2012, 44 per cent trusted their local MP to tell the truth compared with 30 per cent for MPs in general.[4] This suggests that individual MPs have something to gain from developing their reputation locally. But unfortunately, this may not translate into a positive effect on the reputation of the House as a whole.

The desire to increase public awareness and understanding of the work of the House of Commons is what lies behind the fantastic increase in public outreach and engagement activity that MPs and parliamentary staff have undertaken over the past decade. In the year to March 2020, when Covid-19 abruptly closed down participation activity, there were over 300,000 visitors to the parliamentary estate (including school-age children) and outreach visits reached over 150,000 people in the community.[5] Such activity certainly increases awareness of and knowledge about parliament, and may provide the individuals involved with more reasons to trust MPs. As a 2010 report on trust in politics argued: 'engendering a greater familiarity with politics, politicians and parliament, and building on the more positive views people already have of their local experiences may offer the best chance of success [in building trust]'.[6] But such interventions alone are unlikely to be enough to tackle low levels of public confidence in parliament.

The public focus on behaviour not outcomes

Information sharing and outreach are unlikely to shift the dial on the public's opinion of the House of Commons significantly because most members of the public do not conduct an objective assessment of the outcomes that it achieves against its role as an institution. They do not look at the percentage of select committee recommendations accepted by government, note the range of important amendments made to legislation following MPs' interventions or appreciate the variety of topical debates proposed by backbenchers, unless these matters happen to relate directly to their personal interests. Instead, the public's view of the House of Commons is shaped by the behaviour of individual parliamentarians. That is why every scandal – large or small – has a far more significant impact on the reputation of the House of Commons than any of the positive contributions parliamentarians make to the running of the country.[7]

The public's focus on the behaviour of parliamentarians rather than results they achieve is exacerbated by the tendency of the media to concentrate on bad behaviour rather than subtler good-news stories which do not make for such good headlines. But the way in which MPs respond to such stories can also aggravate the harm that they cause.

When the media reports examples of bad behaviour, it is all too common for politicians to dismiss them as the exception rather than the rule – to decide that something is a one-off and therefore does not really matter. Take, for example, Dame Margaret Beckett's assertion that the outcome of Brexit should 'trump' the allegations of harassment and failure of leadership made against the Speaker John Bercow during the 'Pestminster' scandal.[8] Her comment is evidence of why bullying and harassment have never been effectively addressed in Westminster. It was also an unusually honest articulation of the actual priorities of too many politicians – who are prepared to overlook their colleagues' ineffectiveness or poor behaviour when political considerations are in play. Boris Johnson's decision not to discipline Priti Patel after an independent inquiry had found she had bullied civil servants is another example. Politicians like Beckett and Johnson (and the other MPs who supported their positions) tend to assume that their view of the pre-eminent importance of politics is universally held; they forget it is they who are the unusual minority within the population in engaging directly with party politics. To the public, such instances are yet more examples of the attitude of 'one rule for us and another for them', which creates a dangerous distance between members and those who elect them.

Nor is it the case that 'one-off' problems are as unimportant as some MPs tell themselves. Every reported misdemeanour by an individual MP, every example of MPs acting as if rules do not apply to them, chips away at public respect for the House of Commons in a way which is not easy to repair. Confirmation bias is a powerful force, and the public have been primed to expect the worst from their politicians. It is depressing how often politicians carelessly confirm their suspicions.

Dismissing incidents as 'one-off' also tends to mean ignoring larger issues of which they may be a symptom. Following the MPs' expenses scandal, it was briefly recognised that the culture which encouraged inappropriate claims on public funds had arisen partly from the tendency of House of Commons staff to defer to the bullying demands of a minority of unpleasant and entitled MPs. In the aftermath of the crisis, staff – of whom I was one at the time – were reminded that their role was to act as guardians of the House of Commons as an institution as well as servants of current MPs.

But the effect was short-lived. A decade later, Dame Laura Cox described a deferential, subservient culture in which bullying behaviour was allowed to thrive.[9] The power imbalance between elected politicians and unelected staff which had facilitated inappropriate use of expenses was the same as that which enabled some MPs to mistreat with impunity those who worked with them. A new regulator (IPSA) and system for paying expenses had addressed the specific problem of expense claims – which was important – but had not tackled the underlying cultural issue.

An exemplar not an exception

Instead of making excuses for poor behaviour and allowing political considerations to override the desirability of reforms to the House of Commons, MPs should recognise the importance of embracing them. Too often, MPs refer to the uniqueness of the House of Commons to justify their resistance to change. The Commons is unique in some ways, and for some good reasons, but too often this is simply used as an excuse for inertia.

The emphasis on MPs' unique status has negative consequences for MPs themselves. MPs are not protected from discrimination at work because they are not employees or workers under the definition in the Equalities Act. Nor are they personal or public office holders (because elected public offices are excluded by the Act). Female MPs who become pregnant have no automatic right to maternity leave – unlike ministers, they have no employment from which they can take leave, and no employer capable of allowing leave.

The House of Commons should turn this culture of exceptionalism on its head. MPs should aspire for their institution to be an exemplar instead of an exception, modelling the highest possible standards as a workplace and as an employer. If MPs want other employers to follow the laws they make, they need to demonstrate they think they are worth following themselves. A modern parliament would provide MPs with the same rights as employees across the country and find pragmatic solutions to the practical problems this might raise. Other parliaments, including the Swedish Riksdåg, have managed to do so: Westminster trails behind. And when individual MPs do not meet appropriate standards of behaviour, there need to be visible consequences – not special treatment intended to protect allies and preserve political advantage, as the public saw with the Owen Paterson scandal.

It is not just the social but also the physical fabric of parliament which should meet the highest standards. And once again this should not just mean preserving history but adapting to changing circumstances and seizing opportunities to increase the effectiveness and accessibility of the legislature for the public it represents. Too often, the unique history of the Palace of Westminster is used as justification for a disinclination to adapt and improve the building.

When parliament was rebuilt after the catastrophic fire in 1834, it preserved several surviving medieval elements such as the eleventh-century Westminster Hall and the sixteenth-century Cloister Court – and was neo-gothic in style. But it was modern and innovative as a building, ventilated by a state-of-the-art stack system powered by steam boilers, topped with the pioneering technology of cast-iron roofs and decorated with tiles produced by newly developed encaustic methods. MPs today should emulate the approach of their Victorian forebears. The R&R programme should be grasped as an opportunity to envision a parliament equipped for the twenty-first century, not simply to preserve the innovations of nineteenth-century visionaries which have now been surpassed, or worse, abandoned altogether.

The past is not a guarantor for the present

Westminster's long history shapes its built environment but also its procedures. The House of Commons is respected internationally for its long history, which means that it is seen as an important source of procedural expertise and precedent. Parliamentarians and staff of other legislatures often visit, eager to learn from the long history of one of the world's oldest parliaments.

But longevity does not necessarily confer superiority. Commons procedures have been distorted over the last century and a half to meet the requirements of modern governments pursuing legislative programmes for which they claim electoral mandates. Over time, parliamentary procedure has become fundamentally undemocratic because it has become excessively complex. This means MPs do not operate on a level playing field, and even interested members of the public are unable to understand what is being done in their name. MPs should establish permanent mechanisms for periodic review of the procedures and practices of the House of Commons and revision of the standing orders which underpin them, to ensure they are as comprehensible, succinct and effective as possible.

Just as MPs should not be satisfied to rely on the history of the House of Commons as grounds for its modern reputation, nor should they succumb to the assumption that Westminster is already an exemplar in all things. That this is a fallacy was most recently highlighted by the effective ways in which other parliaments coped with the restrictions imposed by the Covid-19 pandemic.[10] The Brazilian legislature, for example, already had a sophisticated system for remote voting and online participation in scrutiny and law-making processes in place – something that Westminster had to develop from scratch when the pandemic arrived. The Senedd was the first UK parliament to hold a virtual plenary meeting. Westminster demonstrated an impressive ability to innovate at speed at the start of the pandemic but also strong reactionary tendencies – with the government being determined to return everything as fast as possible to the previous status quo. Many other legislatures have adopted the best of the innovations made during the pandemic to permanently enhance their proceedings. MPs should look to other parliaments – to the Senedd in Wales, the Scottish parliament and the Northern Ireland Assembly and other legislatures – for ways to improve their own procedures and practices. When it comes to the House's administration, MPs should look beyond other legislatures to examples of other complex organisations in order to find models of best practice they might emulate.

The present should not prejudice the future

If the history of the House of Commons is not necessarily a good guide to how the organisation should be run today, then the preferences of current MPs may not be the best guide to what the House will need in the future. As discussed in Chapter 5, the governance structures of the House of Commons are almost entirely focused on the needs and desires of current MPs, which means that they are incapable of bringing any strategic focus to bear on the long-term interests of the House as an institution. Constitutionally, it can only be today's elected members who make decisions about the running of the House of Commons, but it would be a mistake to believe that the inclinations of a current majority are identical to the longer-term interests of the institution.

This has been demonstrated again and again by the failure of successive generations of MPs to progress the restoration and renewal of the Palace of Westminster. The House of Commons Commission's recommendation, in early 2022, that MPs axe the Sponsor Body and take the 'client' function back in-house, is the latest depressing backward step. If a full decant is abandoned, the consequences are likely to be catastrophic – in the form of a major fire, a death from falling masonry or a lengthy unplanned evacuation as ancient mechanical and electrical systems finally give way. MPs should also make greater efforts to take the longer-term interests of the House of Commons into account and review rules and working practices which may limit the diversity of future MPs.

Democratic inside as well as out

Most importantly, if the House of Commons is to reform itself, it must address the inappropriate degree of control over its procedures and processes exercised by whichever party is in government. This imbalance creates a disjuncture between its public image as a bastion of democracy, and the reality: that its internal practices often fail to meet democratic standards of inclusiveness, equality and protection for minority rights.

Under the doctrine of parliamentary sovereignty, MPs themselves are responsible for decisions about how the House of Commons is run. In theory, MPs can initiate reforms they think might make it run better. But in practice, majority governments can use their control over the agenda and decisions of the House of Commons to ensure that their own conceptualisation of 'the good of the House' prevails. The SNP MP Pete Wishart told me: 'Parliament could be incrementally improving itself all the time, but it can't because government is in control.'

It is an unequal battle. Governments are focused on protecting their own interests within parliament and have resources and mechanisms to deploy to this end. But the House of Commons itself has no individual or body within it that can stand up for it or speak on its behalf. The House's governance structures are diffuse, and leadership is often lacking, because it is simply the sum of its members. This means that there is no one whose role it is to focus on maximising the day-to-day effectiveness of the House or its long-term interests, including its public reputation.[11]

The Commons does have various leadership positions and committees, but each must defer to or rely on others in order to get things done. The Leader of the House is the government minister responsible for the relationship between government and the House of Commons, responsible for ensuring that the government's legislative programme is successfully delivered, but also representing the House of Commons in government. The balance that a Leader strikes between these two roles has a dramatic effect on the likelihood of reform ideas being able to progress. Some – like Jacob Rees-Mogg – appear to focus almost entirely on pursuing the government's interests in parliament, while others – like the late Robin Cook – more evidently champion the interests of the House.

The Speaker plays an important representative role on behalf of the House but is chosen by MPs to chair its debates and to keep order – not to act as a Chief Executive. He or she must act in accordance with the House's will – as Speaker William Lenthall said when Charles I stormed into the Commons chamber to arrest five members: 'I have neither eyes to see, nor tongue to speak in this place, but as the House is pleased to direct me, whose servant I am here.' The Speaker has a limited power to initiate reflection – through working groups or Speaker's Conferences. But he or she has no ability to ensure that the recommendations of such initiatives are implemented.

The House of Commons Commission (discussed in Chapter 5) is perhaps the body one might expect to make strategic decisions on its behalf, but it has no statutory duty to look after the long-term interests of the Commons. Normally the Commission is too bogged down with the minutiae of the management of parliamentary services and the firefighting of emergencies to see much beyond the current parliamentary session. Longstanding SNP member of the Commission, Pete Wishart, told me: 'The Commission is always in reactive mode responding to crises – coronavirus, bullying, R&R.'

The government should not have a majority on the House of Commons' governance committees and their backbench members should be elected rather than appointed.[12] This would allow MPs with a genuine interest in the running of the House to put themselves forward and give the proposals brought forward by these committees greater credibility among members. More lay members should be appointed to the Commission, to ensure that the wider interests of the public carry greater weight against those of current MPs and political parties, and one of the non-executive members should be the chair. The papers the Commission receives should be published and its discussions should be fully recorded so that the public can see how decisions about the running of their parliament have been reached. And importantly, the Commission should be given a statutory duty to act in the long-term interests of the House of Commons as an institution, and to ensure that the proceedings and premises of the House are fully accessible.

But alone, changing the membership and operating practices of the key governance committees will not be enough to ensure that ideas for reforming the Commons can become reality. Cross-party committees regularly come up with proposals to improve the House's scrutiny, debate or law-making functions. But as discussed in Chapter 3, governments can readily prevent such proposals from being adopted – most easily by declining to schedule opportunities for them to be debated and voted upon. There are no means for back-benchers to compel the government to allow the House to make a decision. Often it is only some kind of high-profile incident that can force them up the agenda, as when outrage over the then chairman of the Conservative party, Brandon Lewis MP, breaking a 'pairing' arrangement with the Liberal Democrat MP Jo Swinson on a key Brexit vote forced the government to allow proxy voting to be piloted.

Numerous recommendations for reform of the House of Commons languish unconsidered because governments have not seen it as in their interests to let them be discussed. Others have been discussed and agreed to, but remain unimplemented, waiting for the government to schedule consideration of the necessary motions to bring them into effect. Depressingly, the leaderships of opposition parties are often complicit in this inaction, with an eye to their own interests when they are next in power.[13]

The government's excessive control over the House of Commons is detrimental to its public reputation. First, it means that possible reforms that could make the Commons more effective or more attractive to prospective MPs are not adopted. Second, the public sees that the government can limit the scrutiny to which it is subject, creating doubts about its motives. Third, it makes the Commons seem weak in comparison to government – unable to give effect to its own preferences. In the longer term this executive dominance of parliament may backfire by undermining public trust in government itself.

The pandemic has amply demonstrated the extent of executive control over the House of Commons and in particular the way in which majority governments can prevent the House from adopting reforms which ministers think are not in their interests. An example was the government's approach to remote voting, which had been introduced at the start of the pandemic. Despite protests from the Procedure Committee, the opposition and backbench MPs, the government allowed temporary rules allowing remote voting to lapse, then held an *in-person* vote to set up its preferred in-person voting system on a day when over two hundred MPs who were quarantining, shielding or caring for dependants were not in Westminster. This disenfranchised the very MPs who were most likely to object to the return of in-person voting, breaching the fundamental democratic principle of equality in decision making. Later in June, the government conceded that 'clinically vulnerable' or 'extremely vulnerable' MPs should be able to participate in oral questions and ministerial statements virtually, but it was not until 30 December 2020 – when it was expedient for the government to allow all MPs to participate in the passage of key Brexit legislation – that it allowed virtual participation in legislative proceedings again. This meant that the most medically vulnerable MPs were prevented by the government from participating in the scrutiny of laws for two-thirds of 2020. Conservative MP Tracey Crouch, who was undergoing treatment for breast cancer, made headlines when she challenged the way she had been prevented from participating in a debate on that very subject.

The pandemic has also demonstrated wider problems with government control over the House of Commons. The academics Meg Russell, Ruth Fox, Ronan Cormacain and Joe Tomlinson have argued that the government's approach to legislating during the pandemic, combined with weak parliamentary control over enormous public spending on Covid-19, the denial of equal rights to MPs to participate in proceedings and the mass use of proxy votes, 'Collectively ... amount to a fundamental undermining and exclusion of parliament and its members from crucial decisions – on policy, spending, and the management of the House of Commons itself.'[14]

It should not be so easy for the government to prevent reforms being discussed or adopted. This could be addressed by introducing a requirement for regular debates on topics chosen by the Liaison or Procedure committees – perhaps once every quarter – so the government could not prevent proposals being considered. These debates should be on motions which give MPs the opportunity to vote on the proposals put forward, and the convention against the overt or covert whipping of 'house business' should be scrupulously observed so that no government can be accused of skewing the playing field in its own favour.

The Commons needs a crisis

In this book I have argued that the House of Commons needs to reverse the vicious cycle of declining public trust into which it has fallen – a downward spiral which has been accelerated by the twin crises of Brexit and Covid-19. But I have also shown that it is not simply in the gift of MPs to address the various issues that I have identified; the extent of executive control over parliament means that the government needs to be on board for any reform to happen. In practice most initiatives for change will not succeed unless they are actually launched by ministers, as when Norman St John-Stevas pushed forward reforms of the select committee system in 1979, or Gordon Brown initiated the Wright review in 2009, because MPs and committees lack the means to take the initiative. But the incentives for government to instigate reform are absent because most of the shortcomings of the House of Commons operate in its favour.

The academic and former MP Tony Wright has argued that in this context, achieving reform in parliament 'is a matter of exploiting cracks and getting wedges into doors', together with 'Relentless pressure and ingenuity on the part of those who want to strengthen parliament'.[15] It is with the intention of helping to create that pressure that I have proposed reforms to the House of Commons which would help improve public trust in the institution and nurture executive respect for its role.

But realistically I know that the changes I have proposed are unlikely to come about. At present there is neither the will amongst MPs nor the incentive for the government to rebalance control of the agenda between the executive and backbenchers, or subject legislation to more thorough scrutiny.

Although reforms to public policy outlined in parliament by government are normally presented as necessary, welcome and progressive, changes in the way parliament itself is run are often portrayed (by those with a vested interest in the status quo) as alarming, risky and inherently unappealing.

'It's like wading through treacle', Sarah Wollaston MP told me. During her final year as Chair of the Liaison Committee she managed to push through a small change to select committee procedure – to allow one committee to invite one or more members of other committees to join their evidence-taking sessions. This licence to temporarily increase the breadth of a committee's expertise – known as 'guesting' – was used to great effect to enhance scrutiny of the government's response to the Covid-19 crisis. But – Wollaston said – getting past all the procedural hurdles to make even small changes just 'sucked all the oxygen out of the room'. Powerful interests in preserving the status quo create resistance to even the smallest alterations to the way things are done, let alone more radical ideas.

Many academics have written about the role of crises in facilitating far-reaching institutional change, and sadly the history of the House of Commons aligns precisely with the literature which argues that significant change only happens following a crisis.[16] Unfortunately perhaps, what the House of Commons needs is a crisis to open a 'window of opportunity' in which reform can happen – a disaster which could form a turning point in the House's downward spiral. Maybe only such a crisis can jolt MPs collectively and the government in particular out of their complacency, compelling them to acknowledge the strength of public unhappiness with the way they are currently 'doing' politics and forcing them to identify and act to rectify the shortcomings of the House of Commons.

The MPs' expenses scandal was enough to trigger wholesale reform of the expenses system – the question is, what it would take to generate a similarly comprehensive revitalisation of Westminster politics? It seems neither the travails of Brexit nor the challenges of Covid-19 were enough. Ironically, perhaps MPs' failure to progress the R&R project will end up being the trigger for comprehensive reforms. If the unmodernised palace finally goes up in flames like the cathedral of Notre Dame, parliamentarians will find themselves forced out of Westminster without notice. The task of re-creating parliament in such circumstances would prompt reflection on many previously unthinkable questions about the way our politics operates. Perhaps it is only such a disaster that will force Westminster to reverse the cycle of decline into which it has fallen.

Notes

Introduction

1 Prorogation marks the end of a parliamentary session. It is the formal name given to the period between the end of a session of Parliament and the state opening of parliament that begins the next session. During prorogation almost all parliamentary activity ceases.

2 'R (on the application of Miller) (Appellant) *v* The Prime Minister (Respondent) Cherry and others (Respondents) *v* Advocate General for Scotland (Appellant) (Scotland)' (2019), United Kingdom Supreme Court, case 41.

3 'Parliament and Brexit', UK in a Changing Europe (23 March 2020), accessed 2 September 2021, https://ukandeu.ac.uk/wp-content/uploads/2020/03/Parliament-and-Brexit-report.pdf.

4 Members of the House of Lords can question Lords ministers and require responses to the reports of their committees.

5 Hugh Gaitskell, *In Defence of Politics* (London: Birkbeck College, 1954).

6 Eurobarometer: Public opinion in the European Union, European Values Study and European Social Survey, all accessed 2 September 2021, https://europa.eu/eurobarometer/screen/home; https://europeanvaluesstudy.eu/; www.europeansocialsurvey.org.

7 'Public Perceptions of Standards in Public Life in the UK and Europe', Committee on Standards in Public Life (March

2014), accessed 5 September 2021, www.gov.uk/government/ publications/public-perceptions-of-standards-in-public-life-in-the-uk-and-europe.

8 Greg Power, *Global Parliamentary Report 2012: the changing nature of parliamentary representation* (UNDP and IPU 2012), accessed 5 September 2021, www.ipu.org/resources/ publications/reports/2016–07/global-parliamentary-report-2012-changing-nature-parliamentary-representation.

9 Onora O'Neill, *What we don't understand about trust*, TEDxHousesOfParliament (June 2013), accessed 8 September 2021, www.ted.com/talks/onora_o_neill_what_we_don_t_understand_about_trust?language=en.

10 R.S. Foa, A. Klassen, D. Wenger, A. Rand and M. Slade, *Youth and Satisfaction with Democracy: Reversing the Democratic Disconnect?*, Centre for the Future of Democracy (October 2020), accessed 6 September 2021, www.cam.ac.uk/system/ files/youth_and_satisfaction_with_democracy.pdf.

11 Anne Applebaum, *Twilight of Democracy: The Failure of Politics and the Parting of Friends* (London: Allen Lane, 2020), p. 115.

12 Philip Norton, 'Is the House of Commons Too Powerful? The 2019 Bingham Lecture in Constitutional Studies, University of Oxford', *Parliamentary Affairs* 72:4 (2019), 996–1013.

13 Peter Riddell, *Parliament under Pressure* (London: Weidenfeld & Nicolson, 1998).

14 Jess Sergeant, 'Co-ordination and divergence: devolution and coronavirus', *Institute for Government*, 29 October 2020, accessed 4 June 2021, www.instituteforgovernment.org.uk/ publications/devolution-and-coronavirus.

15 Many of these referendums have been on questions relating to devolution – ten sub-national referendums since the early 1970s have been used to ask whether particular areas of the UK want to introduce additional layers of government. There have also been three UK-wide referendums since 1973, on EEC membership (1975), the parliamentary voting system (2011) and EU membership (2016).

16 'Report of the Independent Commission on Referendums: Executive summary, conclusions and recommendations', University College London Constitution Unit (July 2018), accessed 6 September 2021, www.ucl.ac.uk/constitution-unit/

sites/constitution-unit/files/EC_and_C_and_R_-_ICR_Final_
Report.pdf.

17 HC Deb [House of Commons Debate (Hansard)] 9 January
2019, vol 652, col 367.

18 Parliament itself has expressed concern about this. See
correspondence between the House of Lords Secondary
Legislation Scrutiny, Delegated Powers and Regulatory
Reform and Constitution Committees and Leader of
the House of Commons, Jacob Rees-Mogg, in October
2020, https://committees.parliament.uk/committee/255/
secondary-legislation-scrutiny-committee/publications/3/
correspondence/.

19 It is telling how often MPs mistakenly refer to the Westminster
parliament as the 'mother of parliaments'. When the politician
and reformer John Bright coined this phrase in 1865, he was
referring to England – the country which had exported its
'Westminster model' of democracy throughout the British
Empire.

20 Laura Cox, *The Bullying and Harassment of House of
Commons Staff: Independent Inquiry Report* (15 October
2018), p. 4, accessed 6 September 2021, www.parliament.uk/
globalassets/documents/conduct-in-parliament/dame-laura-
cox-independent-inquiry-report.pdf.

Chapter 1

1 The Health Protection (Coronavirus, Restrictions) (England)
(Amendment) (No. 2) Regulations 2020.

2 Although the constitutional lawyer Tom Hickman QC has
questioned whether the use of the urgency procedure was
justified at all. See Tom Hickman, 'A very English lockdown
relaxation', *UK Constitutional Law Blog*, 14 May 2020,
accessed 6 September 2021, https://ukconstitutionallaw.org.

3 Meg Russell, Ruth Fox, Ronan Cormacain and Joe Tomlinson,
'The marginalisation of the House of Commons under Covid
has been shocking; a year on, parliament's role must urgently
be restored', *Constitution Unit Blog*, 21 April 2021, accessed
6 September 2021, https://constitution-unit.com/2021/04/21/
covid-and-parliament-one-year-on.

4 Samuel Osborne, 'New coronavirus laws are "error-strewn" and confusing, human rights lawyer warns', *Independent*, 24 September 2020.

5 House of Lords Select Committee on the Constitution, 'COVID-19 and the use and scrutiny of emergency powers' (HL 2019–21, 15).

6 Tom Hickman, 'Abracadabra law-making and accountability to Parliament for the coronavirus regulations', in Paul Evans, Christine Salmon, Paul Silk and Hannah White (eds), *Parliaments and the Pandemic* (Study of Parliament Group, January 2021).

7 Ronan Cormacain, 'Unaccountability – the Disease within Government', *UK Constitutional Law Association Blog*, 17 May 2021, accessed 18 September 2021, https://ukconstitutionallaw.org.

8 Meg Russell and Philip Cowley, 'The Policy Power of the Westminster Parliament: The "Parliamentary State" and the Empirical Evidence', *Governance: An International Journal of Policy, Administration, and Institutions* 29:1 (2016), 121–137.

9 A recent body of academic research has disputed the argument that the UK parliament is ineffective and weak. My own research has shown the wide range of types of impact that committees can have on government. (Hannah White, 'Select committees under scrutiny: The impact of parliamentary committee inquiries on government', *Institute for Government*, 9 June 2015, accessed 6 September 2021, www.instituteforgovernment.org.uk/publications/select-committees-under-scrutiny).

10 Meg Russell and Meghan Benton, 'Selective Influence The Policy Impact of House of Commons Select Committees', *University College London Constitution Unit*, June 2011, accessed 6 September 2021, www.ucl.ac.uk/constitution-unit/sites/constitution-unit/files/153.pdf.

11 Other recommendations are never even made because the government is prompted to change its policy by the progress of a committee inquiry.

12 Catherine Haddon, 'Parliament, the Royal Prerogative and decisions to go to war', *Institute for Government*, 6 September 2013, accessed 6 September 2021, www.instituteforgovernment.org.uk/blog/parliament-royal-prerogative-and-decisions-go-war.

13 'R (on the application of Miller and another) (Respondents) *v* Secretary of State for Exiting the European Union (Appellant)' (2017) United Kingdom Supreme Court, case 5.

14 Meg Russell and Daniel Gover, *Legislation at Westminster: Parliamentary Actors and Influence in the Making of British Law* (Oxford: Oxford University Press, 2017).

15 Nicholas Watt, 'Tax credits vote: PM accuses Lords of breaking constitutional convention', *Guardian*, 26 October 2015.

16 'Ministers Reflect: Harriet Harman', *Institute for Government*, 19 May 2017, accessed 6 September 2021, www.instituteforgovernment.org.uk/ministers-reflect/person/harriet-harman.

17 House of Lords Select Committee on the Constitution, 'Fast-track Legislation: Constitutional Implications and Safeguards' (HL 2008–09, 116), para. 152.

18 Joe Marshall, Alice Lilly, Maddy Thimont Jack and Hannah White, 'Parliamentary Monitor 2020', *Institute for Government*, 20 May 2020, p. 42, accessed 6 September 2021, www.instituteforgovernment.org.uk/sites/default/files/publications/parliamentary-monitor-2020.pdf.

19 Jeff King, 'Looking Back at the EU Future Relationship Act', *University College London Europe Blog*, 11 January 2021, accessed 6 September 2021, https://ucleuropeblog.com/2021/01/11/looking-back-at-the-eu-future-relationship-act.

20 'Strathclyde Review: secondary legislation and the primacy of the House of Commons', Cm 9177 (December 2015).

21 House of Lords Select Committee on the Constitution, 'The Legislative Process: The Delegation of Powers' (HL 2017–19, 225), para. 52.

22 House of Lords Select Committee on the Constitution (HL 2019–21, 71).

23 A decision of the Department for Business, Energy and Industrial Strategy challenged in the courts by the campaign group the Good Law Project.

24 This was achieved using a procedure known as an 'Humble Address' – a formal request to the Queen to direct her ministers to give the documents to Parliament.

25 'PM statement on Brexit' (20 March 2019), accessed 6 September 2021, www.gov.uk/government/speeches/pm-statement-on-brexit-20-march-2019.

26 Meg Russell, 'Brexit and Parliament: The Anatomy of a Perfect Storm', *Parliamentary Affairs* 74:2 (2021), 443–463.

27 Even after the 2017 election – arguably a fresher representation of the 'will of the people' than the referendum – in which voters withdrew support from Theresa May's government to the extent that she could only govern having struck a 'confidence and supply' agreement with the Democratic Unionist Party, the political strength of the mandate from the referendum was sustained.

28 Damien Gayle, 'Brexit: suspending parliament should not be ruled out, says Dominic Raab', *Guardian*, 8 June 2019.

29 This five-week suspension would have left just two sitting weeks before the 31 October Brexit deadline, a final fortnight during which much of Parliament's time would have been taken up by the formalities which follow a prorogation (a state opening of parliament, Queen's Speech and week-long debate).

30 The same arguments had been made against a bill introduced by backbenchers Oliver Letwin and Yvette Cooper, which became law against the government's wishes in April 2019 – with the aim of forcing the government to seek an Article 50 extension.

31 Anthony H. Birch, *Representative and Responsible Government* (London: Allen & Unwin, 1964).

32 HC Deb 4 September 2019, vol 664, col 291.

33 Nor did the Prime Minister apparently see the value of parliament ever meeting in September – as it normally does each year. A handwritten note scribbled on the bottom of the memorandum described September sittings as a 'rigmarole' introduced by David Cameron to show that MPs were 'earning their crust'.

34 As Theresa May did not have a Commons majority, she entered into a deal with the Democratic Unionist Party – providing additional funding to Northern Ireland in return for their MPs' support on the most important Commons votes. This significantly complicated the politics of Brexit because the DUP's unionist policy platform was threatened by possible negotiation outcomes.

35 Ciaran McGrath, '"They've undermined trust in democracy!" Tory MP Halfon says time to kick out Remainers', *Express*, 30 October 2019.

36 HC Deb 25 September 2019, vol 664, col 774.

37 HC Deb 25 September 2019, vol 664, col 660.

38 David Blood, Oliver Elliott and John Burn-Murdoch, '"Toxic" tweets aimed at MPs soar after Johnson outburst', *Financial Times*, 27 October 2019.

39 Frances Perraudin and Simon Murphy, 'Alarm over number of female MPs stepping down after abuse', *Guardian*, 31 October 2021.

40 Paul Evans, Paul Silk and Hannah White, 'Afterword' in Evans et al. (eds), *Parliaments and the Pandemic*, pp. 200–208.

41 The government began these on 16 March – nine days before the Commons rose for its Easter recess – and held them daily for the next 92 days, before moving to a more ad hoc approach from 23 June. The Prime Minister also made several televised addresses to the nation.

42 'Procedure under coronavirus restrictions', Oral evidence taken by the House of Commons Procedure Committee on 8 June 2020, HC 300, Q.103 to 106. During the 2019–21 parliamentary session, DHSC received 7,850 questions for 'ordinary answer' (normally answered within seven days) and 5,862 'named day' questions (for answer by a specific date). This was more than twice as many questions as the next highest department, the Treasury (3,238 ordinary and 2,657 named day questions), which also played a key role in the government's pandemic response. Figures from Alice Lilly, Hannah White, Paul Shepley, Jess Sargeant, Kwabena Osei and Samuel Olajugba, *Parliamentary Monitor 2021*, Institute for Government, September 2021, accessed 18 September 2021, www.instituteforgovernment.org.uk/sites/default/files/publications/parliamentary-monitor-2021.pdf.

43 'Coronavirus Statutory Instruments Dashboard' *Hansard Society*, accessed 6 September 2021, www.hansardsociety.org.uk/publications/data/coronavirus-statutory-instruments-dashboard#total-coronavirus-sis.

44 *Ibid.*

45 Cormacain, 'Unaccountability – The Disease within Government'.

46 Owen Bowcott, 'Ex-lord chief justice: UK parliament must scrutinise Covid rules', *Guardian*, 28 September 2020.

47 Hickman, 'Abracadabra law-making'.

48 The amendment agreed to the extension of the powers "provided Ministers ensure as far as is reasonably practicable that in the exercise of their powers to tackle the pandemic... Parliament has an opportunity to debate and to vote upon any secondary legislation with effect in the whole of England or the whole United Kingdom before it comes into effect."

49 HC Deb 30 September 2020, vol 681, col 331.

50 Hannah White, 'Against the Clock: Brexit, COVID-19 and the Constitution', Bingham Lecture in Constitutional Studies given at Balliol College, Oxford, 18 May 2021, www.law.ox. ac.uk/events/bingham-lecture-against-clock-brexit-covid-19-and-constitution.

51 Meg Russell, 'Should we worry if MPs seize control of the parliamentary agenda?', *Constitution Unit Blog*, 27 January 2019, accessed 6 September 2021, https://constitution-unit.com/2019/01/27/should-we-worry-if-mps-seize-control-of-the-parliamentary-agenda-where-could-that-lead-politics.

52 Robert Saunders, 'Prorogation struck at the very heart of parliamentary democracy. But it was not an isolated incident', *Mile End Institute Blog*, 22 July 2020, accessed 6 September 2021, www.qmul.ac.uk/mei/news-and-opinion/items/prorogation-struck-at-the-very-heart-of-parliamentary-democracy-but-it-was-not-an-isolated-incident-dr-robert-saunders.html.

53 'R v The Prime Minister' (2019).

Chapter 2

1 HC Deb 9 September 2019, vol 664, col 497.

2 Matthew Smith, 'Are MPs elected to exercise their own judgement or do their constituents' bidding?', *YouGov* (13 August 2019), accessed 6 September 2021, https://yougov.co.uk/topics/politics/articles-reports/2019/08/13/are-mps-elected-exercise-their-own-judgement-or-do.

3 HC Deb 9 September 2019, vol 664, col 464.

4 Matt Chorley, 'Delegate or representative, what is an MP really for?', *Times*, 1 February 2019.

5 Philip Cowley, 'What makes a Tory MP rebel – and what are their red lines on Brexit?', *London School of Economics Blog*, 3 July 2017, accessed 3 September 2021, https://blogs.lse.ac.uk/

brexit/2017/07/03/what-makes-a-tory-mp-rebel-and-what-are-their-red-lines-on-brexit.

6 See, for example, Tom Brake, 'MPs – Delegates or Representatives?' *The House*, 20 June 2018, accessed 6 September 2021, politicshome.com/thehouse/article/mps–delegates-or-representatives.

7 The number would have been higher still if the government had not adopted a strategy of making concessions and delaying the passage of legislation when defeats looked likely. See Marshall et al., 'Parliamentary Monitor 2020', p. 38.

8 Rowena Mason and Heather Stewart, 'Daily Telegraph "Brexit mutineers" front page blamed for threats to MP', *Guardian*, 15 November 2017.

9 Membership of the Conservative, Labour and the Liberal Democrat parties declined to a historic low of 0.8 per cent in 2013 before increasing to around 1.7 per cent of the electorate in 2019, according to the House of Commons Library (Lukas Audickas, Noel Dempsey and Philip Loft, 'Membership of UK Political Parties: Standard Note 05125', *House of Commons Library* (9 August 2019), accessed 6 September 2021, https://commonslibrary.parliament.uk/research-briefings/sno5125).

10 Geoffrey Evans and Florian Schaffner, 'Brexit identities: how Leave versus Remain replaced Conservative versus Labour affiliations of British voters', *The Conversation*, 22 January 2019.

11 'Audit of Political Engagement 16: the 2019 Report', *Hansard Society* (2019), accessed 6 September 2021, www.hansardsociety.org.uk/publications/reports/audit-of-political-engagement-16.

12 Hannah Pitkin, *The Concept of Representation* (Berkeley: University of California Press, 1967), p. 209.

13 Rosie Campbell, Sarah Childs and Joni Lovenduski, 'Do Women Need Women Representatives?', *British Journal of Political Science*, 40:1 (2010), 171–194. https://doi.org/10.1017/S0007123409990408.

14 Eleonora Alabrese, Sascha O. Becker, Thiemo Fetzer and Denis Novy, 'Who voted for Brexit? Individual and regional data combined', *European Journal of Political Economy*, 56 (2019), 132–150.

15 Tanya Abraham, 'Two in five oppose measures to improve MP diversity', *YouGov* (22 November 2019), accessed 6 September 2021, https://yougov.co.uk/topics/politics/articles-reports/2019/11/22/two-five-oppose-measures-improve-mp-diversity.

16 And a second law giving some women the right to vote.

17 'Women in Parliament 1995 to 2020: 25 years in review', *Inter-Parliamentary Union*, 2020, accessed 6 September 2021, www.ipu.org/resources/publications/reports/2020–03/women-in-parliament-1995–2020–25-years-in-review.

18 'Women in Parliament in 2018: The year in review', *Inter-Parliamentary Union*, 2019, accessed 6 September, www.ipu.org/resources/publications/reports/2019–03/women-in-parliament-in-2018-year-in-review.

19 Eliot Chappell, '51% of Labour MPs are women. What now for all-women shortlists?', *LabourList*, 31 October 2019, accessed 6 September 2021, https://labourlist.org/2019/12/51-of-labour-mps-are-women-what-now-for-all-women-shortlists.

20 Including Oxford West and Abingdon, Totnes, Gosport and Bracknell.

21 Elise Uberoi, Carl Baker, Richard Cracknell, Grahame Allen, Nerys Roberts, Cassie Barton, Georgina Sturge, Shadi Danechi, Rachael Harker, Paul Bolton, Rod McInnes, Chris Watson, Noel Dempsey and Lukas Audickas, 'General Election 2019: results and analysis, Second edition: Briefing Paper 8749', *House of Commons Library* (28 January 2020), accessed 6 September 2021, https://commonslibrary.parliament.uk/research-briefings/cbp-8749. Elise Uberoi and Rebecca Lees, 'Ethnic diversity in politics and public life: Briefing Paper 01156', *House of Commons Library* (23 October 2020), accessed 6 September 2021, https://commonslibrary.parliament.uk/research-briefings/sno1156.

22 This has consequences for the representation of women in positions of political responsibility. Following the 2019 election, Boris Johnson was criticised for the low numbers of female MPs in his Cabinet. Government press conferences during the Covid-19 pandemic were dominated by men, prompting concern about the diversity of voices contributing to decision-making in government.

23 In evidence to the Procedure Committee inquiry into *Procedure under Coronavirus restrictions* Daisy Cooper MP chose to discuss her hidden disability: 'I would like to add my perspective as an MP with a hidden disability ... I have Crohn's disease and ... What that means for me personally is that every single day I have to constantly juggle what I eat, how much I eat, when I eat, how much water I drink – all these kind of things – alongside managing my pain management and my diary ... As far as I am concerned, call lists have been revolutionary for me personally, and I think would be for many other people with long-term illnesses and long-term conditions.' 'Procedure under coronavirus restrictions', Oral evidence taken by the House of Commons Procedure Committee on 8 June 2020 (HC 300, Q.319).

24 'Election of single-figure disabled MPs 'disappointing''', *Disability Rights UK* (17 December 2019), accessed 6 September 2021, www.disabilityrightsuk.org/news/2019/december/election-single-figure-disabled-mps-disappointing.

25 As the populations of Scotland, Wales and Northern Ireland are made up of 5.4 per cent, 5.9 per cent and 2.2 per cent minority ethnic groups, respectively. The numbers in the House of Lords are even worse – just 6.3 per cent of peers are from minority ethnic groups.

26 Andrew Reynolds, 'The UK's parliament is still the gayest in the world after 2019 election', *Pink News*, 13 December 2019, accessed 6 September 2021, https://www.pinknews.co.uk/2019/12/13/uk-gay-parliament-world-2019-general-election-snp-conservatives-labour-lgbt.

27 Reliable data on the proportion of the population that is lesbian, gay, bisexual or transgender was gathered for the first time via the Census in 2021, with members of the public asked to provide information about their sexual orientation and gender identity.

28 Christopher Watson, 'House of Commons trends: The age of MPs: Library Insight', *House of Commons Library* (3 November 2020), accessed 6 September 2021, https://commonslibrary.parliament.uk/house-of-commons-trends-the-age-of-mps.

29 Luke Audickas and Richard Cracknell, 'Social background of MPs 1979–2019: Briefing Paper 7483', *House of Commons*

Library (27 March 2020), accessed 6 September 2020, https://commonslibrary.parliament.uk/research-briefings/cbp-7483.

30 'Elitist Britain 2019: the educational backgrounds of Britain's leading people', *Sutton Trust and Social Mobility Commission* (24 June 2019), accessed 6 September 2021, www.gov.uk/government/publications/elitist-britain-2019.

31 Richard Clegg, 'Graduates in the UK labour market: 2017', *Office for National Statistics* (24 November 2017), accessed 6 September 2021, www.ons.gov.uk/employmentandlabourmarket/peopleinwork/employmentandemployeetypes/articles/graduatesintheuklabourmarket/2017.

32 'Parliamentary Privilege 2019: Educational backgrounds of the new House of Commons' (13th December 2019), *Sutton Trust*, accessed 6 September 2021, www.suttontrust.com/wp-content/uploads/2019/12/Parliamentary-Privilege-2019–1.pdf.

33 Chrysa Lamprinakou, Laura Morales, Virginia Ros, Rosie Campbell, Maria Sobolewska and Stuart Wilks-Heeg, 'Diversity of candidates and elected officials in Great Britain: Research report 124', *Equality and Human Rights Commission*, March 2019.

34 *Speaker's Conference (on Parliamentary Representation)*, *House of Commons* (11 January 2010), HC 239-I, para 6.

35 Sarah Childs, 'The Good Parliament', University of Bristol, July 2016, accessed 6 September 2021, www.bristol.ac.uk/media-library/sites/news/2016/july/20%20Jul%20Prof%20Sarah%20Childs%20The%20Good%20Parliament%20report.pdf.

36 Campbell et al., Do Women Need Women Representatives?'

37 Harriet Harman, 'Speaker's Lecture Series 2018 – Women in British Politics – Where Next?', 22 October 2018. www.harrietharman.org/speaker_s_lecture_series_2018_women_in_british_politics_where_next.

38 Submission from The Fawcett Society (SC-67) to the Speaker's Conference (on Parliamentary Representation) (2 April 2009), accessed 6 September 2021, https://publications.parliament.uk/pa/spconf/167/167we77.htm.

39 See, for example, Pamela Paxton; Melanie M. Hughes and Tiffany D. Barnes, *Women, Politics, and Power: A Global Perspective* (Lanham, MD: Rowman & Littlefield, 2020).

40 HC Deb 30 November 2020, vol 685, col 127–134.

41 HC Deb 10 March 2021, vol 690, col 150–175WH.

42 HC Deb 8 June 2020, vol 677, col 47.

43 *Speaker's Conference (on Parliamentary Representation).*

44 Sonika Sethi, Aditi Kumar, Anandadeep Mandal, Mohammed Shaikh, Claire A. Hall, Jeremy M. W. Kirk, Paul Moss, Matthew J. Brookes and Supratik Basu, 'The UPTAKE study: implications for the future of COVID-19 vaccination trial recruitment in UK and beyond', *Trials*, 22:296 (2021).

45 Rosie Campbell and Philip Cowley, 'What Voters Want: Reactions to Candidate Characteristics in a Survey Experiment', *Political Studies*, 62:4 (2014), 745–765.

46 Abraham, 'Two in five oppose measures to improve MP diversity'.

47 Julia Hollingsworth, Krystina Shveda, Natalie Leung, Denis Bouquet and Henrik Pettersson, 'New Zealand has just elected one of the most diverse parliaments in the world. Here's how it stacks up', *CNN*, 17 November 2020.

48 *Speaker's Conference (on Parliamentary Representation).*

49 The Liberal Democrat party voted to adopt every measure made available in the 2016 Act, in an effort to increase the diversity of its MPs.

50 'Improving Parliament. Creating a better and more representative House', *All Party Parliamentary Group for Women in Parliament* (July 2014), accessed 6 September 2021, http:// appgimprovingparliamentreport.co.uk/download/APPG-Women-In-Parliament-Report-2014.pdf.

51 Elise Uberoi, 'Coronavirus: MPs' use of virtual participation and proxy voting by gender: Insight', *House of Commons Library* (10 December 2020), accessed 6 September 2021, https://commonslibrary.parliament.uk/coronavirus-mps-use-of-virtual-participation-and-proxy-voting-by-gender.

52 'Parenting in lockdown: Coronavirus and the effects on work-life balance', *Office for National Statistics* (22 July 2020), accessed 6 September 2021, www.ons.gov.uk/peoplepopulationandcommunity/healthandsocialcare/conditionsanddiseases/articles/parentinginlockdowncoronavirusandtheeffectsonworklifebalance/2020-07-22.

53 This followed earlier problems experienced by the Labour MP Naz Shah (21 June 2018) and Liberal Democrat MP Jo Swinson (17 July 2018).

54 During the pandemic, the right to a proxy vote was extended to any MP unable to vote in person.

55 The UK parliament is not alone – inclusivity is one of the three themes emphasised by the Inter-Parliamentary Union, the global membership organisation for national parliaments – in its analysis of what needs to be done to improve the 'gender-sensitivity' of legislatures around the world.

56 'The Jackdaw', *The Mace weekly newsletter* (by email), 27 November 2020.

57 Ashley Cowburn, 'Majority of ethnic minority MPs have experienced racism at Westminster, survey suggests', *Independent*, 17 February 2020.

58 Opportunities to reshape the chamber arose following the fire of 1834 and the bombing of the chamber during the Second World War.

59 Robert Shrimsley, 'Adversarial cultures obstruct real change', *Financial Times*, 14 May 2010.

60 As parliamentary clerks Chloe Challender and Harriet Deane explored in the context of the Covid-19 pandemic ('The construction of the "Good Parliamentarian"', in Evans et al., *Parliaments and the Pandemic*, pp. 134–144).

61 Rowena Mason and Peter Walker, '"Surrender act": Johnson ignores calls to restrain his language', *Guardian*, 29 September 2019.

62 Nicola Woolcock, 'Abuse puts girls off a career in politics, says Oxford High head teacher', *Times*, 30 January 2021.

63 'Intimidation in Public Life A Review by the Committee on Standards in Public Life', Cm 9543 (December 2017).

64 Hannah White, 'Abusive politics and the exodus of women MPs', letter to the Editor, *Times*, 1 November 2019.

Chapter 3

1 Lisa James and Meg Russell, 'Parliament, spin and the accurate reporting of Brexit', *Constitution Unit Blog* (24 October 2019), accessed 6 September 2021, https://constitution-unit.com/2019/10/24/parliament-spin-and-the-accurate-reporting-of-brexit/.

2 BBC Newsnight interview with Steve Baker (19 October 2019), accessed 6 September 2021, www.youtube.com/watch?v=iFhZhD8wAFY.

3 Raphael Behr, 'This house is no longer a fit home for British democracy', *Prospect*, 12 December 2019.

4 Alexander Fanta, 'The real story why "bonkers Brussels" went bananas', *EU Observer*, 5 October 2020.

5 'Greensill: What is the David Cameron lobbying row about?', *BBC News*, 9 August 2021, accessed 6 September 2021, www.bbc.co.uk/news/uk-politics-56578838; 'Owen Paterson: Minister Stephen Barclay expresses regret over vote', *BBC News*, 9 November 2021, accessed 19 December 2021, www.bbc.co.uk/news/uk-politics-59213255.

6 These proposed amendments are intended to be a prompt for discussion – as clerks are not trained in legal drafting (that being the job of a small group of specialised government lawyers), their drafts are rarely in the form needed to be made into law. If an MP succeeds in persuading the government of the merit of an amendment (which happens relatively rarely) or gets a majority of MPs to vote for it against the wishes of the government (even rarer), then the government will normally give an undertaking to introduce a properly drafted amendment at a later stage.

7 This was the rule of which Conservative rebels fell foul in June 2021, when they tried to force the government to honour its manifesto commitment to spend 0.7 per cent of Gross National Income on international aid by amending the unrelated Advanced Research and Invention Agency Bill.

8 This was an innovation which proved particularly valuable once Covid-19 arrived. According to analysis by the House of Commons Library, 325 MPs cast their votes by proxy at some point between 11 June and 3 November 2020 (Elise Uberoi, 'Coronavirus: MPs' use of virtual participation and proxy voting by gender: Insight', *House of Commons Library* (10 December 2020), accessed 6 June 2021, https://commonslibrary.parliament.uk/coronavirus-mps-use-of-virtual-participation-and-proxy-voting-by-gender/).

9 Mark Hutton, David Natzler, Matthew Hamlyn, Colin Lee, Chloe Mawson, Crispin Poyser, Eve Samson and Kate Lawrence, *Erskine May: Parliamentary Practice 25th Edition* (London: LexisNexis Butterworths, 2019).

10 Bercow reinterpreted the meaning of the parliamentary term 'forthwith', which would normally have prevented an amendment being considered.

11 HC Deb 9 January 2019, vol 652, col 372.

12 See https://erskinemay.parliament.uk.

13 See https://guidetoprocedure.parliament.uk/mps-guide-to-procedure.

14 The EVEL rules were subsequently repealed in July 2021.

15 The language and process of the humble address – a request to the Queen for her ministers to share information with parliament – seemed archaic. But the fact that MPs should have a mechanism for requiring the Executive to release information to the legislature should be uncontroversial.

16 HC Deb 18 March 2019, vol 656, col 775.

17 See for example Jack Maidment, 'How John Bercow used an archaic parliamentary rule from 1604 to thwart Theresa May's Brexit deal', *Telegraph*, 8 March 2019. The proceedings were even covered as far afield as the US by the *Washington Post*.

18 See the responses to the Speaker's statement (HC Deb 18 March 2019, vol 656, col 776–792).

19 Mark D'Arcy, 'Modernising rows', *BBC News*, 21 May 2014, accessed 6 September 2021, www.bbc.co.uk/news/uk politics-27505650.

20 Although the paper-based system remains available for those who prefer it.

21 Cristina Leston Bandeira, 'Parliamentary petitions and public engagement: an empirical analysis of the role of e-petitions', *Policy & Politics*, 47:3 (2019), 415–436.

22 Hugo Gye, 'Remainer revolt: fury as senior Commons official "secretly plots with Tory rebels to derail Brexit"', *Sun*, 20 January 2019.

23 D'Arcy, 'Modernising rows'.

24 Robert Hazell and Fergus Reid, 'Private Members' Bills', in Cristina Leston-Bandeira and Louise Thompson (eds), *Exploring Parliament* (Oxford: Oxford University Press, 2018), p. 126.

25 House of Commons Procedure Committee, 'Private Members' Bills' (HC 2015–16, 684).

26 Another disadvantage of the Procedure Committee is of capacity – its members have limited time and must prioritise examining the most high-profile procedural questions which arise – for example, during 2018 and 2019 dealing with questions arising from the Brexit process.

27 Proposals for reform of Commons Standing Orders developed in 2014 have yet to be implemented. By comparison, the Scottish Parliament last revised its rules in 2016–17, the Canadian House of Commons in 2017, the Australian House of Representatives in 2018 and the New Zealand House of Representatives in 2019–20.

Chapter 4

1 HC Deb 23 June 2020, vol 677, col 1247.
2 HC Deb 23 June 2020, vol 677, col 1261.
3 HC Deb 23 June 2020, vol 677, col 1250.
4 See, for example, the apology made by Ian Paisley, Jr MP in which he said, 'I am disappointed that I was not able to persuade members of the Committee of the weight of my arguments on some of the major matters of mitigation, especially on the issue of paid advocacy. However, I accept the report, but I do so regret its sanctions.' HC Deb 19 June 2018, vol 645, col 589.
5 In the end the vote was not formally whipped, although the *Guardian* reported that 'Tory whips told their MPs that the chief whip would be voting against the Bryant amendment and for the motion in the name of the leader of the house' (Alexandra Topping, 'Rees-Mogg loses vote to let MPs debate bullying claims', *Guardian*, 23 June 2018).
6 'Note from Dame Laura Cox ahead of the debate on 23 June 2020', accessed 6 September 2021, www.parliament.uk/globalassets/documents/commons-governance-office/dame-laura-cox-note-ahead-of-23-june-2020-debate.pdf.
7 However, one of the first ICGS cases highlighted an inconsistency with wider standards processes: the Conservative MP Rob Roberts was suspended for six weeks for harassing a member of his staff, but his suspension did not trigger a recall petition, as a breach of the Members' Code of Conduct would have done.
8 Campbell and Cowley, 'What Voters Want'.
9 Hutton et al., *Erskine May*, para 12.1.
10 The privilege of free speech was put into law in Article IX of the 1689 Bill of Rights, which states that 'the freedom of

speech and debates or proceedings in Parliament ought not to be impeached or questioned in any court or place out of Parliament'.

11 In theory, in order to ensure they can attend the House of Commons to do their job, MPs also benefit from the privilege of freedom from arrest for civil matters. In practice, the likelihood of this privilege ever being exercised in modern times is extremely slim.

12 However, the fact that the Executive is nearly always formed from a political party with a majority of MPs in the House of Commons means that in practice it can normally exert its will on the House by whipping its members to support its business.

13 As confirmed in 2010 by the Committee on Issue of Privilege ('First Report: Police Searches on the Parliamentary Estate' (HC 2009–10, 62), 22 March 2010.

14 Claire Ellicott, Ben Spencer and Alex Ward, 'One Rule for Them!', *Daily Mail*, 2 October 2020.

15 Jack Peat, 'Cameron lobbying suggest there are "different rules" for Tories – Dodds', *London Economic*, 13 April 2021.

16 Subject to the discretion of the chair and the right of parliament to legislate. The Commons rule was confirmed in resolutions of the House of 23 July 1963 and 28 June 1972.

17 A further consequence of the Cash for Questions scandal was the passage, in 1996, of the Defamation Act, which included provisions delineating the boundaries of parliamentary privilege. The act allows an MP to waive privilege in order to refer to statements they have made in the House when giving evidence in a court of law.

18 'MPs' freedom of information cover-up is a dark day for democracy', *Evening Standard*, 18 May 2007.

19 Ben Worthy, 'Freedom of information and the MPs' expenses crisis', in Jennifer vanHeerde-Hudson (ed.), *The Political Costs of the 2009 British MPs' Expenses Scandal* (Basingstoke: Palgrave Macmillan, 2014).

20 Andrew Sparrow, Hélène Mulholland, Richard Partington and Patrick Wintour, 'More than 50 MPs flipped second home, new expenses figures show', *Guardian*, 20 December 2009.

21 Matthew Parris, 'The Pathology of the Politician', *Spectator* (May 2011).

22 HC Deb 16 July 2020, vol 678, col 1740.

23 Disappointingly, the rumour that it is illegal to die in the Palace of Westminster turns out to be a myth ('Legal curiosities: fact or fable?', *Law Commission*, March 2013, accessed 5 July 2020, www.lawcom.gov.uk/app/uploads/2015/03/Legal_Oddities.pdf).

24 'Procedure under coronavirus restrictions', Oral evidence taken by the House of Commons Procedure Committee on 5 October 2020 (HC 300, Qs. 282–283).

25 The *New York Times* reported that 'Britain's Parliament was a bit like Disneyland, but without the fun' (Stephen Castle, 'They're Calling It the "Conga Line Parliament"', *New York Times*, 2 June 2020).

26 Matthew Smith, 'Only 12% of Brits think MPs should have to physically be in Commons to vote during COVID-19 crisis', *YouGov*, 3 June 2020, accessed 6 September 2021, https://yougov.co.uk/topics/politics/articles-reports/2020/06/03/only-12-brits-think-mps-should-have-physically-be-.

27 'Procedure under coronavirus restrictions', (HC 300, Q.11).

Chapter 5

1 Lucy Fisher, 'Fallen angel causes alarm at crumbling Westminster', *Times*, 20 April 2018.

2 'Parliament investigates report of falling masonry', *BBC News online*, 19 October 2017, accessed 21 December 2021, www.bbc.co.uk/news/uk-politics-41684109.

3 Jonathan Owen, 'Parliament refurbishment will cost at "least £12bn", chair of spending watchdog says', *Building*, 19 January 2021.

4 Charles Goodsell, 'The Architecture of Parliaments: Legislative Houses and Political Culture', *British Journal of Political Science*, 18:3 (1988), 288.

5 Alex Meakin, *Understanding the Restoration and Renewal of the Palace of Westminster: An analysis of institutional change in the UK Parliament.* PhD thesis, University of Sheffield, 2019.

6 Charlotte Higgins, '"A tale of decay": the Houses of Parliament are falling down', *Guardian*, 1 December 2017.

7 Richard Rogers, 'The Welsh Assembly', in Design Commission, *Designing Democracy* (London: Policy Connect, 2015), pp 13–14.

8 John Bercow, 'Designing for Democracy' *Parliamentary Affairs* 71:4 (2017), 845–852.

9 Another project beset by obstruction and delay, as described by the historian Caroline Shenton in her 2016 book *Mr Barry's War* (Oxford: Oxford University Press).

10 'Fires (2019)', *House of Commons Freedom of Information Disclosures*, accessed 6 September 2021, www.parliament.uk/site-information/foi/foi-and-eir/commons-foi-disclosures/estates-information/fires-2019.

11 'Further details about fires in House of Lords areas', *House of Lords Freedom of Information Disclosures*, accessed 6 September 2021, www.parliament.uk/globalassets/documents/foi/house-of-lords-foi-and-data-protection/foi-responses—calendar-year-2020/foi-3381—response.pdf.

12 Benjamin Kentish, 'House of Commons leak: debate called off after water pours into chamber', *Independent*, 4 April 2019.

13 Joint Committee on the Palace of Westminster, 'Restoration and Renewal of the Palace of Westminster' (2016–17, HL 41 HC 659), para 57.

14 The tiles are made by a specialist manufacturer in Shropshire using a traditional nineteenth-century method of pouring coloured liquid clay into a mould, then firing the pattern onto the tile base using a kiln. Their installation is undertaken by stonemasons from a specialist conservation contractor.

15 Joint Committee on the Palace of Westminster, 'Restoration and Renewal of the Palace of Westminster', Chapter 3, Table 5.

16 'Restoration and Renewal Programme: Strategic Review', *Houses of Parliament Restoration and Renewal* (March 2021), accessed 7 September 2021, https://restorationandrenewal.uk/resources/reports/strategic-review.

17 HC Deb 16 July 2020, vol 678, col 1736.

18 Robin Ibbs, 'House of Commons services: report to the House of Commons Commission', *House of Commons Commission*, 28 March 1990, p. 5.

19 Matthew Flinders, Leanne-Marie McCarthy-Cotter, Alix Kelso and Alex Meakin, 'The Politics of Parliamentary Restoration and Renewal: Decision, Discretion and Democracy', *Parliamentary Affairs* 71:1 (2018), 144.

20 Alexandra Meakin, 'Palace of Westminster Restoration and Renewal – a new era, or more of the same?', *Hansard Society Blog*, 7 April 2020, accessed 7 September 2021, www.hansardsociety.org.uk/blog/palace-of-westminster-restoration-and-renewal-a-new-era-or-more-of-the-same.

21 'Restoration and Renewal Programme: Strategic Review', *Houses of Parliament Restoration and Renewal.*

22 'The cost of coronavirus', *Institute for Government* (January 2021), accessed September 7 2021, www.instituteforgovernment.org.uk/explainers/cost-coronavirus.

23 Tony Wright, 'Prospects for Parliamentary Reform', *Parliamentary Affairs*, 57:4 (2004), 874.

24 HC Deb 16 July 2020, vol 678, col 1748.

25 The House of Commons Commission is a statutory body – established by the House of Commons Administration Act 1978. In 2015 the House of Commons Commission Act added that the Commission 'must from time to time set strategic priorities and objectives in connection with services provided by the House Departments'.

26 In recent years, questions considered by the Commons Administration Committee have included: what cutlery should be used in members' dining rooms (2015), whether Acts of Parliament should be printed on vellum (2015), what support Members should receive after an election (2017) and how the House should respond to the Covid-19 pandemic (2020).

27 The most recent lyings-in-state have been those of King George VI in 1952, Queen Mary in 1953, Sir Winston Churchill in 1965 and Queen Elizabeth, the Queen Mother in 2002.

28 Flinders et al., 'The Politics of Parliamentary Restoration and Renewal'.

29 Matthew Flinders, Alex Meakin and Leanne-Marie McCarthy Cotter, 'The double-design dilemma: political science, parliamentary crisis and disciplinary justifications', *Journal of Legislative Studies*, 25:2 (2019), 250–277.

30 Childs, 'The Good Parliament'.

31 Karen Ross, 'Women's Place in "Male" Space: Gender and Effect in Parliamentary Contexts', *Parliamentary Affairs*, 55:1 (2002), 189–201.

32 HC Deb 31 January 2018, vol 635, col 939.

33 'Restoration and Renewal Programme: Strategic Review', *Houses of Parliament Restoration and Renewal.* p. 18.
34 HC Deb 20 May 2021, vol 695, col 909.
35 Russell et al., 'The marginalisation of the House of Commons under Covid has been shocking'.
36 HC Deb 25 March 2021, vol 691, col 1181.

Conclusion

1 OECD, 'Trust and Public Policy: How better governance can help rebuild public trust', *OECD public governance reviews* (Paris: OECD Publishing, 2017).
2 After dropping to a low point of 59.4 per cent in 2001, voter turnout in UK general elections has gradually recovered – reaching 67.3 per cent of eligible voters in the 2019 election – although remaining some way short of the 1950 peak of 83.9 per cent. The Brexit referendum in 2016 saw a 72.2 per cent turnout (Lukas Audickas, Richard Cracknell and Philip Loft, 'UK Election Statistics: 1918–2019: A Century of Elections: Briefing Paper 7529', *House of Commons Library* (February 2020)).
3 Norton, 'Is the House of Commons Too Powerful?'
4 *Survey of public attitudes towards conduct in public life 2012*, Committee on Standards in Public Life (September 2013). After 2012 funding for the surveys was, sadly, withdrawn by the government.
5 'The House of Commons: Administration Annual Report and Accounts 2019–20', *House of Commons* (21 July 2020, HC 580).
6 Ruth Fox, *'What's trust got to do with it? Public Trust in and Expectations of Politicians and Parliament'*, Hansard Society, Political Studies Association and the Centre for Citizenship, Globalisation and Governance (2010).
7 Norton, 'Is the House of Commons Too Powerful?'
8 'Dame Margaret Beckett says Brexit issues "trump bad behaviour"', *BBC News*, 16 October 2018, accessed 7 September 2021, www.bbc.co.uk/news/av/uk-politics-45884222. This comment was especially dispiriting coming from a member of the Committee on Standards in Public Life – the body charged with monitoring standards of behaviour across the public sector.

9 Cox, *The Bullying and Harassment of House of Commons Staff.*

10 Evans et al., *Parliaments and the Pandemic.*

11 As Sarah Childs has argued, 'the historic preference for regarding MPs as individual office-holders reflects the individual mandate Members receive from the electorate. This in turn explains the apparent reluctance of them to embrace an institutional identity, making it harder for Members to accept a collective responsibility' (Childs, 'The Good Parliament').

12 My research has shown that elected chairs and members have more credibility with their peers and are more motivated to do a good job when they have an electoral mandate for their roles, than when they owe their position to the government (White, 'Select committees under scrutiny').

13 One idea that could shift the balance of control over the House of Commons away from the government is an example of one which has been agreed to, but not unimplemented. The Wright Committee proposed the idea of a House Business Committee, a cross-party group which would meet each week to agree the House's agenda for the next. Gordon Brown, the then Prime Minister, agreed that the proposal would be brought forward in the 2010 Parliament. Following the election, the Coalition Agreement explicitly promised that 'A House Business Committee, to consider government business, will be established by the third year of the [2010] Parliament', but this promise was never fulfilled.

14 Russell et al., 'The marginalisation of the House of Commons under Covid has been shocking'.

15 Tony Wright, 'Reforming Parliament', *Prospect*, 23 October 2004.

16 See, for example, John Keeler, 'Opening the window for reform mandates, crises, and extraordinary policy-making', *Comparative Political Studies*, 25:4 (1993), 433–486 and Andrew Cortell and Susan Peterson, 'Altered states: explaining domestic institutional change', *British Journal of Political Science*, 29:01 (1999), 177–203.

Index